A typical burst through by Supermac. Malcolm Macdonald leaves the Arsenal defence standing.

Watch out! Ian Hutchinson is about.

News of the World FOOTBALL AND SPORTS ANNUAL

Edited by Frank Butler

WORLD DISTRIBUTORS (MANCHESTER) LIMITED

CONTENTS

*Published in Great Britain by News of the World
and World Distributors (Manchester) Limited
12 Lever Street, Manchester M60 1TS*

*For the use of certain photographs we acknowledge
with thanks: Ken Adams,* Angling Magazine, *Associated Press, Butlins, Central Press Photos,
County Press Photos Lancs., Patrick Eagar,
Keystone Press, London Photo Agency, London
Weekend TV, Terry Lake, Harvey Ormeshan,
Photocall Features, Planar Press, Sportspix,
Sport and General, Dave Steuart, Press
Association Photos, Syndication International,
Raymonds News Agency, Press Agency, Yorks.,
SKR Photos International.*

Book layout by Pamela Mara

*Printed in Great Britain by
Fletcher & Son Ltd, Norwich*

NEWS OF THE WORLD
WORLD'S LARGEST SUNDAY SALE
SOCCER BONANZA! Banks...O'Farrell...Nicholson: See Pages

INTRODUCTION
by
FRANK BUTLER
(Sports Editor, News of the World)

It's seven years since we presented the first *News of the World Football and Sports Annual*, and it's good to know it's as popular as ever. This year we've kept up our high standard of presenting the biggest names in sport.

Alan Ball (Arsenal), Stan Bowles (Queen's Park Rangers), Norman Hunter (Leeds United) and Ray Clemence (Liverpool) have all written special articles.

Reg Drury has picked out six soccer stars who hit the headlines last season. He has presented profiles of Martin Dobson (Burnley), Roger Davies (Derby County), Phil Parkes (Queen's Park Rangers), Dave Watson (Sunderland), Dave Clements (Everton) and Tommy Hutchison (Coventry City).

Jimmy Hill, the man you see on the box every week, and, of course, read his views weekly in the *News of the World*, is again featured.

Jimmy, who has switched from London Weekend to B.B.C., is one of the most influential men in soccer. Some top clubs consult him and he is also a consultant to the Football Association.

Reg Drury, Terry McNeill and Don Evans head the *News of the World* team of top Soccer Writers with special articles.

All the other popular sporting features of the *News of the World* are, of course, included. Johnny Leach, twice former world table tennis champion, gives splendid advice to young players. Jack Wood deals with golf while Brian Harris passes on his great knowledge of fishing.

There is another sports quiz and once again I'll be glad to receive more of your letters with any suggestions you care to make. I hope you again enjoy the efforts of the *News of the World*'s sports team.

A goal for Stan Bowles and Gerry Francis.

YOU'VE GOT TO FIGHT HARD FOR SUCCESS

by STAN BOWLES

(Queen's Park Rangers)

There must be plenty of youngsters around who could have been playing professional football instead of watching it every Saturday.

I admit that you need luck to make it at that level, but you also need encouragement and belief in yourself.

It's easier to say to yourself when things are going wrong: 'I'm not going to bother. It's not worth all the trouble.'

I know that's right because I was in that position myself. There were occasions when I thought it was all a waste of time and my advice to kids is that if you believe you have the ability, stick at it, train hard and make people notice you.

My career is a perfect example of how it pays to be persistent. Mind you, I was a bit of a fool when I was younger, but I'm sure there are others like me who should be in the game.

I signed for Manchester City when I was seventeen – that's when Joe Mercer and Malcolm Allison were in charge at Maine Road. I was in the First Division at eighteen and everything was great.

Then I had a row over wages and I said to Joe: 'I want my cards if you won't give me any more money.' And he said that if that's how I felt I'd better go.

Before that I'd had a row with Malcolm over time off and we ended up swinging punches at each other,

Stan Bowles makes a flying leap over Peter Simpson.

so I wasn't too shocked when I was told I could go, even though it was a blow to my pride.

I was on the point of packing it in then. I wondered why I should bother, just like other lads with ability have done. I drifted to Bury and only lasted there a couple of months and it would have been so simple to have felt sorry for myself and got a job outside football.

But I always knew that I had the ability. It was the encouragement and luck I needed and out of the blue I got them both from a man called Ernie Tagg, who was manager of Crewe, an unfashionable club in the Fourth Division.

'Look son,' he told me. 'I am prepared to give you one last chance. If you mess me about, I kick you out on your ear. Don't let me or yourself down because you'll always regret it.'

I didn't let him down. I will always be grateful to Ernie for believing in me, yet I still had to do it myself.

That's what I mean about not taking the easy way out. I put more into my training – and without fitness you are nothing – and set about rebuilding my career.

You need a lot of self-confidence to think that after a series of set-backs and finding yourself in the Fourth Division that you can bounce back.

But I knew inwardly that if I worked hard enough, there was a fair chance that a club from a higher division would buy me. And when Second Division Carlisle agreed a fee of £12,000 with Crewe, I didn't hesitate.

Ernie Tagg was happy. He got me for nothing and made a profit. I was happy because I knew that I'd justified myself and I learned later that Ian McFarlane, then the Carlisle manager, was more than pleased with the way things turned out.

But I was even then determined to get back into the First Division. Carlisle were in the Second and nothing would have suited me more than to have gone up with them.

Ian McFarlane hardly stopped telling me I had what it takes and it's only when you've left and had time to reflect that you realise just what an effect managers have on you.

If they keep giving you confidence, as Ian and Ernie Tagg did, then you're half-way there and now that I'm in the big-time I often think back to the days when I was an impetuous kid.

It could so easily have ended for me when I walked out on Manchester City and I wonder just how many others there are scattered around Britain who could have made the professional game – or even become a top-class amateur – had they had my good fortune.

But I can't stress too strongly that you also need perseverance and dedication. It's a criminal waste of talent when young lads with every chance of success at any level of the game throw it away because they become dispirited.

And if you listen to me, you won't let your chin sag if you can't kick with your right foot as effectively as you can with your left, or in my case, the other way round.

I haven't much use for my right foot, except for standing on, and I haven't found it too big a handicap. So stick at it and you might be surprised at the progress you make.

It's Galloping Stan again jumping over Ian Britton (Chelsea).

A Goalie must

have Luck....

RAY CLEMENCE (Liverpool)

Ability, dedication and a willingness to train hard and keep yourself in peak condition. All these things are essential to become a top-class footballer. But you need a lot of luck as well.

I've gained League championship and U.E.F.A. Cup Winners' medals, played in an F.A. Cup Final and for England in two World Cup qualifying ties. And I'm the first to admit that I've had a full share of any luck that was going.

It all seems quite incredible when I reflect that I didn't even want to be a goalkeeper.

As a schoolboy in Skegness I started as a centre-forward and later played at centre-half, left-half and left-back. Anywhere but in goal – I just didn't fancy the position.

But my opinion wasn't shared by the manager of Cosmos Youth Club. And when we reached the final of a Lincolnshire County competition he persuaded me to play in goal, even though I'd been turning out at full-back in the earlier rounds.

That decision had a big influence on my life. For the game was staged at Scunthorpe United's ground and, despite letting in three goals, I did well enough to impress a Scunthorpe scout on the look-out for local talent.

I was coming up to my seventeenth birthday that summer and preparing to leave school to continue my studies as an accountant. But when Scunthorpe offered me professional terms I took the soccer plunge.

If a League club thought I had a chance of making the grade as a goalkeeper, who was I to argue? I reasoned that if things didn't work out, I could always complete my qualifications in accountancy.

I'm a firm believer that, because of the degree of uncertainty involved in big-time football, every youngster should attempt to have an alternative career.

As it happened, things worked out well for me at Scunthorpe. In that first season I had four games in the Third Division, and was still understudy to the experienced Geoff Sidebottom when the following campaign began.

Then Geoff was injured in only the second match, so I was promoted and played in the remaining forty-four fixtures.

A young goalkeeper can do reasonably well and still have a few nightmare games. If a scout turns up on the 'wrong' day it is sheer bad luck, and that must have happened to many lads with Third and Fourth Division clubs over the years.

I'm glad to say that Liverpool must have watched me on the good days, for in the 1967 close-season – when I was still only eighteen – manager Bill Shankly signed me for a fee reported to be £18,000.

There was a lot to learn at Liverpool, not least of all to improve my goal-kicking, and I served an 'apprenticeship' of more than two and a half seasons before becoming a First Division regular.

I was happy in the Liverpool reserve side. It was a good, all-round team and in each of those seasons we won the Central League title.

Manager Shankly groomed me carefully, and I was given an occasional first-team game. But I didn't exactly set Anfield alight in my début against Swansea in a League Cup-tie.

Admittedly, we won 2–0 . . . but I knew I hadn't played very well. Nothing seemed to go right. There was a gale-force wind blowing in my face in the first half and my goal-kicks hardly got off the ground.

A goalkeeper must never be kidded by a result. He can keep a clean sheet and still realise he has had a bad game. It's equally true, of course, that he can let in five goals and know he isn't at fault – though that's hardly an experience to be recommended.

I'll admit that I wondered if that game against Swansea was going to be my first and last for Liverpool.

In fact, my next chance came in Europe – well, almost. I played in home and away games against Eire club Dundalk in the European Fairs Cup.

Liverpool hardly needed a goalkeeper, for we won 10–0 at Anfield and 4–0 in Dundalk. But there was no real pressure so far as I was concerned and I didn't make a mistake on the few occasions I was called upon.

It was later that same season, after Liverpool had been knocked out of the F.A. Cup at Watford, that Mr Shankly began to re-shape the first-team defence and centre-half Larry Lloyd and I were introduced on a permanent basis.

Above: **A worrying moment for any goalkeeper. Dave Clements (Coventry) has Chelsea's defence stretched.** ***Left:*** **Ray Clemence in typical flying action.**

A year later we got to Wembley, where we were beaten 2–1 in extra time by Arsenal. That was my first F.A. Cup defeat and, I suppose, my greatest disappointment.

But on the way to the Cup Final I had probably my finest game for Liverpool when we beat Spurs 1–0 at White Hart Lane in a sixth-round replay.

There are games when everything comes up trumps for a goalkeeper: so much so that even a 'wrong' move turns out right. And I had one of those nights under the Tottenham floodlights.

There are, unfortunately, bad days as well. Like the home match with Leicester when I misjudged a cross and I headed the ball down to the feet of opposing centre-forward Rodney Fern.

And if there is one sight in the world which causes a goalkeeper's stomach to turn over it is the ball in the back of his own net.

I've one last confession to make – as a schoolboy I was a Manchester United fan. Though, living in Skegness, I only saw them on TV.

Indeed, the only First Division game I watched 'live' before I became a professional was between Leicester and Chelsea at Filbert Street.

Ever since that day I've been an admirer of Chelsea's Peter Bonetti, a tremendously stylish goalkeeper with fantastic reflexes. He rates among the best I've ever seen – but, if I was pressed, I'd have to pick the old maestro Gordon Banks as my No. 1.

The Cup that Cracked an Image

by NORMAN HUNTER (Leeds United)

Sunderland at Wembley in May of 1973, A.C. Milan in Salonika a few weeks later. My club of Leeds United have played in any number of important matches over the years but perhaps those two games were more significant than most in that they, I believe, brought about a change in public reaction to us.

When Leeds were promoted from the Second Division to the First Division way back in the 1963–4 season there were many folk who felt that we were likely to go straight back down again. We did not, of course, but the attitude lingered on.

Instead of going down we, in fact, climbed higher and higher, picking up quite a few trophies in the process, but never, it seemed, a great deal of affection. Perhaps we were to blame for this. We were inclined to be a hard side and one that argued too much with referees.

Indeed, I don't think it would be going too far to suggest that if Leeds lost an important match in those years there were more people smiling at the news than were gnashing their teeth in sympathy.

But then came the back end of the 1972–3 season. First came the Cup Final against Sunderland, the one we lost, remember. It was sensational all over the world of football, one we could well have done without but a result which the rest of the world, loving the underdog, delighted in.

But soon after that Wembley disaster for us came the visit to Greece and Salonika for the European Cup Winners' Cup Final against the A.C. Milan side. I don't know what public opinion was before the game but we were left in no doubt after the match was over – and we had lost again.

Via television the match was seen by millions of football fans throughout the world and I can say without the slightest fear of contradiction that we not only did not deserve to lose but did enough to have won half a dozen other games.

To have still played so well and to have lost our second Final within so short a time did something to the vast majority of the public. They began to show sympathy and understanding towards us. We did not expect favours but we had always felt we'd like a fair assessment of our strengths and skills. It had arrived.

For make no mistake about it, Leeds United, in my time with them certainly, have always had a great deal more skill, both individually and collectively, than a lot of people, who should have known better, gave us credit for. But things, at the end of that summer of last year, were definitely on the turn.

Last season it continued, with report upon report enthusing over the 'new image' Leeds, the side which cut the cackle and got on with the game, reports helped along by our great undefeated run of League games which started in August and ended only in February at Stoke.

I think we made a big move in the right direction when we cut down the protesting and the like to referees. They are only human and I don't suppose for one moment that they enjoyed us nattering at them, certainly I wouldn't have done so had I been in their place.

The elimination of the chat has led, I believe, to an easing of the tensions which may have existed in the past between the officials and the players. In turn, I believe this has not only helped the image of Leeds but assisted the players as well.

One quality which has remained constant with Leeds, never in any danger of change, is the tenacity with which we play. The never-say-die spirit has been instilled into all of us. Just as we gave an early season start to the 'new look' Leeds, so we gave an early start in 1974 to a display of that quality.

I refer, of course, to those two vital F.A. Cup games against Wolves way back in January. Its history now, of course, but you may recall that we could easily have given up the ghost and gone out in the first match of that third round tie, but we did not and got

Right: **Referee has words with Johnny Giles after booking Hunter. Norman protesting again. And Hunter really angry after being tackled toughly.**

Leeds colleagues arguing before Hunter is booked against Everton.

an equaliser in the dying minutes of the game.

In the replay at Elland Road, we did not play as well as we can but we again kept plugging away – and Mick Jones headed in the winner when some early birds were already making their way from the ground.

Any youngster joining the Elland Road staff these days finds magnificent facilities for improving his game and his knowledge of life as well, but he also soon learns the value of tenacity, of never giving up. And that can't be bad for life at large, can it?

No, over the years people have often been proved wrong about Leeds, and about me, of course. I'm hard but fair, and although I have a right leg that some folks call just a swinger, I can still use it efficiently when I have to, but preferably first time. If I have to stop and think about it I'm not too hot on it.

But right or wrong, one thing is certain. I'm grateful for football for giving me the life I've had and I hope I've contributed something to the game in return. But in common with every other player I know, even if I had not been lucky enough to have made my living from the game I'd still have played it for 'free'.

I have a young son, Michael, and a daughter, Claire. I have no idea as yet what young Michael will be when he eventually leaves school, though I hope he has an interest in sport generally, but if he is good enough and keen enough to make a professional footballer then I'll be happy to see him become one.

Some people have suggested the game could dig in a decade. I do not think so. It is not only part of the British way of life, it is a vital part of it. Lone may it continue so, and perhaps some of you are destined to play a part in its future. Good luck, and look after the game. It's deserving of the best.

Where Have All the Entertainers Gone?

by ALAN BALL (Arsenal)

It used to be a common sight. You could walk into any park or playing-field in England and spot a young lad with enough natural ability for a League club to work on.

That isn't nearly as true any more. There just aren't as many kids who want to kick a ball around in their spare time.

They have found other things to occupy them and I find this state of affairs very sad. No, it's more than that, it's worrying for somebody like me who cares desperately about the future of football in this country.

The game is in the hands of youngsters. They are the ones who, in ten or more years, will have the responsibility of keeping football alive as we know it.

So I find it dispiriting that there is a sharp decline in interest among the younger generation. Of course, the breed is far from extinct, but significantly, there are not so many keen kids around.

When I was at junior school, I seldom wanted to do anything else than dribble a football when I was let out of my class and frequently we had games of twenty-five a side.

It's not like that now and the reasons for it are not hard to find. Youngsters need heroes. They need to copy the stars, the characters, players with magnificent skill who excite them.

There is nothing so stimulating for a young lad than to watch individuals and then go home and try to do it themselves. That was certainly true of me and my generation.

When lads see something exceptional, they can't – or couldn't – wait to go out on the local park and try it themselves. They may not have the slightest chance of repeating what they have seen, but that's not important.

What really counts is that kids should have these fantasies. It's necessary that they have their dreams and imagination, but unfortunately, there aren't enough exciting players about these days for youngsters to emulate.

How many First Division players can you think of who can be called personalities? There's Queen's Park Rangers' Stan Bowles, Rodney Marsh, of Manchester City, Leeds captain, Billy Bremner, Mick Channon, the Southampton striker, and Newcastle's scoring machine, Malcolm Macdonald.

There are others and I like to think that I do my share of entertaining, but honestly, you have to stop to think before you name the exciting players.

That's significant because not too many seasons ago practically every club in the First Division boasted a player who had instant crowd-appeal.

What also worries me is that youngsters who have retained their love of the game are having their natural skills coached out of them by their schoolteachers.

Many of these teachers, not all by any means, are not qualified to coach. These guilty teachers tell kids where to run, where to pass and worst of all, do not allow their pupils to think for themselves.

I plead for lads who have what it takes to be taught the basics and then be allowed to think for themselves and to use their instincts.

Alan Ball looks sad after being sent off during the England World Cup match in Poland.

But it's not only teachers who must shoulder the blame. There are coaches in the Football League who take all the imagination out of the game.

They tell professionals they must not do anything off the cuff and that they must conform to a set pattern. I agree that there has to be an overall plan, but not to a degree where players are refused the right to express themselves.

I've been shouted at when I've tried to do something different. I remember sitting on the ball against Manchester City.

It was only a bit of fun, but I was told that it wasn't wanted. But that sort of thing is me. I like to smile as well as win.

And I'm certain that kids want to see the flamboyant players. It's little things like these they remember and as long as they have mastered their art, I don't see anything wrong.

I want more entertainers and less rigid coaching. It isn't too much to ask, is it?

Mike Channon, Southampton's striker, attempts to beat two Leeds defenders Billy Bremner and Jack Charlton.

Rodney Marsh (*left*) and Colin Bell protest against the referee's decision in England *v*. Wales World Cup game.

Soccer ballet. Malcolm Macdonald (Newcastle) leaps above Leeds goalkeeper Dave Harvey.

Champion! Billy Bremner expresses delight after scoring for Leeds. Allan Clarke joins in the fun.

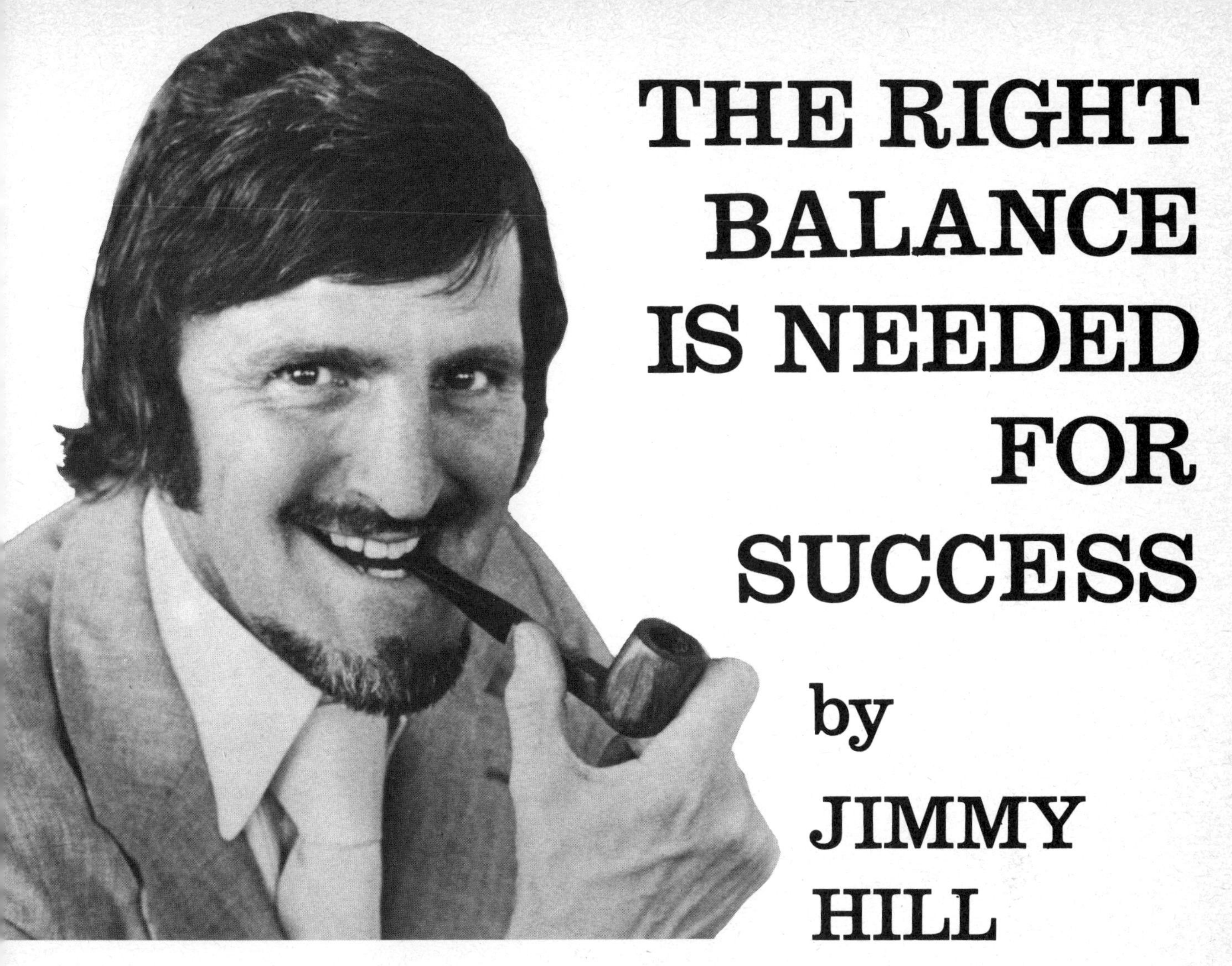

THE RIGHT BALANCE IS NEEDED FOR SUCCESS

by JIMMY HILL

I have come to believe that the most important managerial skill is the ability to balance a football team. By balance I mean getting the right ingredients in every department of a team. In one respect the most unbalanced match I ever saw was between two ladies' teams, one from the Second Generation and the other from the Sportsman Club.

There were only six ladies in each team plus the goalkeepers, John Hollins and Michael Crawford. Both ladies' teams played six forwards attacking throughout and no defenders. That game was unbalanced positionally, but it was most entertaining!

Every team needs to know that enough of its players will be prepared to stay back or get back and defend when the need arises. A few years ago, there were always five forwards and five defenders, but now in professional teams it is seldom that less than six or seven players have defensive responsibilities and often it's as many as nine. From corner-kicks sometimes, all eleven players are back defending the goal.

Another balance to be achieved is that between passing and dribbling. The method and speed with which a team passes the ball from one to the other creates a rhythm and that rhythm in itself persuades players to run into position to invite the next pass.

Obviously, it's necessary to break up that rhythm at times by dribbling an opponent. That helps the whole team, because it makes it far more difficult for the defence to anticipate. Yet, if too many players dribble, or one player dribbles too often, opponents will find it easier to read what is going to happen.

A top team will make at least four or five passes to one dribble, but choosing the right time to take on an opponent is the real art.

A good team also needs enough competitive and aggressive players to make sure that, on a day when things are going wrong, when conditions are impos-

Denis Law leaps over Phil Holder (Spurs).

sibly bad, when luck seems to have disappeared, the team will not collapse.

It takes players who don't drop their own heads, but are going to inspire their colleagues to keep the battle going by their 'never say die' example.

Perfect examples of the kind of player I am talking about are Billy Bremner, Emlyn Hughes and Allan Mullery.

A team has to have enough unselfish players also. Players who will run till they drop for the sake of the side. With the amount of running they do, they may not have enough energy throughout the game, to display pretty skills to the best advantage, but no team can be successful without its share of unselfish running among its players.

Not many people really appreciate the value of good running, and they still tend to assess players who run well as just ordinary. But if you study the way a player like Geoff Hurst continually changes his position, either to make space for himself, or to lure defenders out of the way to make space for others to play, you will know his value and that of players like him.

A standing defender is usually a good defender. If a forward allows him to hold his position, perfectly balanced, ready to move one way or another, then he is more likely to break up attacks than if a forward can find ways of keeping him on the run.

I like a fair share of real pace in a team too. That doesn't mean to say that all eleven have to be sprinters, but there has to be enough pace in all departments of the team, certainly at the front and the back, to get by.

A forward who has sufficient pace is always a menace to a defence. He can create that nagging fear at the back of a defender's mind that, if he should lose him by missing a tackle or misreading a pass, then that's the last he is going to see of him apart from his backside.

Putting that fear into a defence should be a vital part of a team's make-up, and I would hate to put a side on the field that hadn't one or two very quick players to strike into an opponent's penalty area.

The same applies in reverse at the other end. A defender who is able to turn quickly and sprint can

Geoff Hurst attempts to lob one over John Jackson in a Crystal Palace – West Ham clash.

Denis Law scores for Manchester United against Ipswich. George Best looks on approvingly.

afford to make the occasional mistake as his natural speed will so often get him out of trouble.

I am favourably disposed to quick full-backs such as Bob McNab and Paul Madeley, when he plays there, and the best European example is Paul Breitner, the Bayern Munich defender. It doesn't mean to say that you cannot be a full-back if you are not like a greyhound, because that's not so.

There have been more than a few successful full-backs who anticipated and read the play so well that their lack of real speed was seldom exploited. Jimmy Langley, the old Fulham and England player was the best example I know of that.

Yet, with the two centre-backs, I think it is essential that one of them not only has excessive pace, but also has the nimbleness and agility to turn and get under way quickly. I see teams in top-class football playing with two lanky, cumbersome centre-backs and I think it is inviting danger.

There will be matches where it is possible to get away with it, but there will be others where the weakness will be shown up to the full by strikers with agility and pace.

Sufficient skill, is basic to a successful team. Players need enough skill to go with other ingredients. By skill I mean control, the ability to make a variety of accurate passes, the knack of being able to find space as well as the intelligence to read the play and deceive the enemy. Of course, heading and shooting skills have to be there in good measure.

While we are on the subject of heading, I should mention height. Like speed, there should be enough height in a forward line and equally there has to be enough height in a defence, to cope with lofty opponents.

There are players who are not all that tall like Denis Law, who has such a magnificent leap that he can get above far taller players. But on average a good 'big'un' is going to beat a good 'littl'un' in the air, so it helps to have the odd lamp-post-type player in a team, but not too many, please.

A team has to be balanced in the most vital area of football and that is the scoring of goals. Whatever level of football a player plays, over the years he will register a scoring rate. A few years ago some players, very rare ones at that, could muster a goal a game. Jimmy Greaves was in that category.

Nowadays if a striker can average a goal in every two games then, provided he is not over the hill, he is immediately in the £200,000 class.

Some players, though they play in forward positions, seldom score goals and I recognise they may have other qualities which are useful to a team. But, no one should select a team without making account of its scoring rate per match based on the average scoring rate of the players in that team, over the season.

This is not only important for strikers, i.e. those who play in the front three or four, but it's even more important for midfield players. I think it dangerous for a team to expect its front-runners to score all its goals. They are nearly always outnumbered and such is the difficulty of their job under those conditions, that they are bound to have spells when they lose confidence and as a result the goals refuse to come.

That's when it is important to have at least two of the three midfield players able to come up with, maybe, ten to fifteen goals a season. It doesn't need to be twenty or more, but a midfield player should certainly aim at getting himself ten goals a season. It takes so much pressure away from the men up front on days when they are out of scoring luck.

Although I base my argument on top-class teams I am very well aware that a few teams at lower levels are fortunate enough to have a wide variety of good players to choose from. Mostly teams have to be made up from who is available. It is even more important in those circumstances to sit down and weigh up that the most is being made of the playing ingredients that are there.

I know few teams will be lucky enough to have enough of all the necessary ingredients I have mentioned, but on the other hand perhaps there is a hint or two in what I have written that might help you to get a better balance and better results for your team in the coming year.

Billy Bremner holds on to George Eastham's back as Armstrong comes in to take the ball.

ROGER DAVIES ~ An Old-Fashioned Centre-Forward

The term 'striker' is a modern one – applied to front-running players of varying styles whose chief function is to score goals. So Roger Davies, of Derby County, comes into that general category.

But Davies is really an old-fashioned centre-forward: a throwback to the days when the wearer of the No. 9 shirt usually went it alone through a crowded goalmouth, often with his head down.

At times Roger looks ungainly as he pushes and shoves his way through a defence, but he's a deceptive character with uncanny ball-control in a tight situation. And Davies is always ready to have a crack at goal.

He's the kind of centre-forward who is difficult to play against – and, on occasions, not exactly easy to play with. For Roger is so unpredictable he can baffle friend and foe alike; neither know quite what to expect when he has the ball.

There's no doubt Davies has the ability and the courage to reach the very top. He is the man a lot of folk would like to see leading the England attack, and he's a definite contender for a 1978 World Cup place.

In an age when so many First Division players are products of a carefully-coached assembly line, Roger has a refreshing individuality. And he probably owes it to the fact that he was not groomed for stardom from schoolboy days.

It tends to be overlooked that Davies is still something of a novice so far as big-time soccer is concerned. He may have earned a lot of headlines, and even played in eight European Cup-ties in 1972–3, but Roger had made only fifty or so League appearances for Derby at the start of this season.

Roger Davies has a few words with the ref during a Derby County–Spurs cup tie.

Just over three years ago, Wolverhampton-born Davies was turning out each Saturday for a works team and having an occasional trial with a professional club without exciting much interest. It was only when he got his 'big' break, an offer to join Southern League side Worcester City, that Roger began his meteoric rise to the top.

That was at the start of 1971–2, and his unorthodox style not only brought Davies a lot of goals . . . it brought the scouts rushing to Worcester to check on this new 'discovery'.

Wilf Grant, himself a free-scoring centre-forward in the fifties, was manager of Worcester at that stage. Wilf knew he had found a gem. And he wasn't prepared to sell cheaply.

While other League clubs haggled about a price, Derby stepped in to meet Worcester's fee. It was a testimony to the shrewd judgement of Brian Clough and Peter Taylor, and they left Derby no finer legacy than six-footer Davies.

During his initial season at the Baseball Ground, Derby won the League championship for the first time in the club's history. But Roger played no direct part in that triumph. He was proving his worth in the reserve side which also hit the jackpot by winning the Central League.

It was the following season when Davies really 'arrived'. And it was a fourth round F.A. Cup clash with Spurs which made the rest of the soccer world conscious of his arrival.

Roger scored the goal which earned Derby a 1–1 home draw, then emerged as the hero of the White Hart Lane replay when Spurs were beaten 5–3 in extra time. Derby twice fought back after being two goals down, and the big fella notched a spectacular hat-trick.

Roger is my kind of centre-forward. He likes to use his height and weight and he has a tremendous enthusiasm for the game. It's a combination which has already served Derby well, and could lead to a regular England place.

Above: **Roger Davies holds off Chelsea's David Webb.**

Left: **Brian Clough can't stand the strain as he sits on the touchline with Davies.**

DAVE WATSON– the Striker who became Great in Defence

It took six years and an F.A. Cup Final appearance for Sunderland to turn centre-half Dave Watson into an 'overnight success'.

Now Watson has won England recognition and emerged as the first genuine challenger for Roy McFarland's No. 5 shirt since the Derby skipper established himself in the national line-up.

They have a lot in common – though while Dave is

nearly an inch taller and almost a stone heavier than Roy he lacks that vital First Division know-how which only comes from playing regularly against the best strikers in the land.

Watson, in fact, is probably more effective than McFarland as a defender, even if not quite as stylish or as accurate a passer of a ball. But then McFarland is England's finest footballing centre-half since the hey-day of Neil Franklin twenty-five years ago.

Both Dave and Roy also have perfect timing in the air, and each has a reputation for heading goals from corners and free-kicks. Indeed, Watson has proved himself as a centre-forward and was Sunderland's leading scorer three seasons ago.

That very ability to operate either in defence or attack acted as a millstone around Watson's neck for a long time. Sunderland, like his previous club Rotherham, always tended to switch Dave up front when in need of more goal-power.

It says a great deal for Watson's own self-assessment and commonsense that, despite his scoring flair and the glamour that goes with the art of getting goals, he realised that he had a brighter future as a centre-half.

And when Bob Stokoe, himself a former centre-half, took over as Sunderland boss in December 1972, one of his first actions was to promise Watson a permanent place in a No. 5 shirt.

That decision soon paid a handsome dividend for both player and club.

Watson still did his share of the scoring, claiming four of the goals which took Sunderland along the

Life looks good for Dave Watson after Sunderland had won the F.A. Cup.

You takes your choice! Watson holds up the No. 5 and No. 9 shirts which he used to wear with equal accomplishment.

F.A. Cup path to face hot favourites Leeds at Wembley in May 1973. But it was his outstanding display of defensive qualities in the Final, watched by a multi-million TV audience, which did most to emphasise this was no ordinary player.

Sunderland became the first club from the Second Division to capture the trophy in more than forty years, and Watson was generally acknowledged as 'man of the match'.

No neutral spectator was more entitled to a warm glow of self-satisfaction as he listened to the superlatives flow about Watson's performance than Tommy Docherty.

The 'Doc' has pulled off some astonishing transfer deals in his time. But none to better the bargain when, as manager of Rotherham United, he bought Watson from his home-town club Notts County for a fee of less than £1,000 in 1967–8.

Three years later Sunderland complimented Docherty's foresight, by paying £100,000 for Watson. And, in a matter of months, they could have made a handsome profit by selling Dave had they been so inclined.

Chelsea wanted to buy Watson on the eve of the 1971–2 season – and, if successful, intended to play him at centre-forward.

Who knows what Dave could have achieved as a striker with the London club. But it's safe to say that he could not possibly have built a bigger reputation than he has done in his natural centre-half role.

MARTIN DOBSON~ Burnley's Mastermind

Martin Dobson, of Burnley, is twenty-six and he had a long wait to even reach the fringe of the England team. He gained only a single Under-23 cap and it wasn't until November 1973 that he was called up for the full squad.

That was for the Wembley match with Italy which followed immediately after England's elimination from the World Cup by Poland. And though selection acknowledged his international potential, Dobson was simply a spectator that night – he wasn't named for the team or among the five substitutes.

But the best midfield players mature with age, and Martin has the talent and the experience to become the stylist the rebuilt England side will need in the dual bid for the European Nations Cup in 1976 and the World Cup in Argentina two years later.

He has underlined that much as the mastermind of the Burnley side which has re-established itself in the First Division over the past year or so.

Any doubts which lingered about Dobson's ability to raise his performance at the highest League level – and, to be honest, they did exist beyond Turf Moor when Burnley were hitting the Second Division highspots in 1972–3 – have long since been banished.

Martin has not only underlined that he can compete with the best midfield players in the business, he has also proved that – unlike many of his rivals for an England place – he has a genuine goal-flair.

A versatile soccer apprenticeship, in his early days he operated first as a striker and then as a defender, has helped Dobson shine in his present role. His timing in a tackle enables him to win the ball cleanly: he has quick control which aids his accuracy when it comes to passing or shooting.

It has been said that his fault is a tendency to be over-adventurous in putting the emphasis on attack and occasionally neglecting the defensive part of his duties. But even to label that as a 'fault' could be questionable when English football has suffered in recent years from an overdose of safety-first tactics.

There must be a few red faces at Burnden Park, home of Burnley's county rivals Bolton Wanderers, now that Dobson has emerged as a First Division star. Bolton gave Martin a free transfer when he was seventeen, an error of similar proportion to the earlier decision by the same club to release Alan Ball.

Dobson had been a prolific scorer of goals as a schoolboy in his native Clitheroe, so perhaps Bolton expected too much too soon after signing him as a professional. Whatever the reason, they showed him the door after a single season in which he failed to develop into the kind of tearaway striker they had anticipated.

Burnley promptly offered Martin terms, and within four months he was in their League side. And at Turf Moor they were more patient in finding Dobson's true position.

He operated for a spell in defence, winning that

A confident Martin Dobson parades with a happy Sir Alf Ramsey behind him in the England squad.

solitary England Under-23 honour as a centre-half, but it was only a short-term measure in a club crisis. And, in due course, Martin was given the freedom and scope of a midfield role.

Dobson is an elegant footballer, beautifully balanced and with the bonus of finishing power which paid a particularly valuable dividend of eleven goals in Burnley's promotion season.

PHIL PARKES ~ the Goalie Money can't Buy

Phil Parkes, Queen's Park Rangers goalkeeper, must wonder in quiet moments whether to feel elated at his First Division progress or frustrated by the bleakness of his international prospects.

Parkes is rightfully acknowledged as one of the finest 'keepers in Britain. Yet his chances of a quick breakthrough into the England team are hardly bright with Peter Shilton and Ray Clemence, both aged only twenty-five, barring his way.

But you never know what the football future holds . . . and Phil has already proved a number of shrewd judges wrong.

Money couldn't buy Parkes from Q.P.R. Yet when the London club signed him from Walsall for around £15,000 in the summer of 1970 it was not only a shrewd deal on the part of Les Allen, their manager at the time, but confounded those in charge of practically every top club in the Midlands.

Aston Villa, Birmingham City, West Bromwich Albion and Wolves, all near-neighbours of Walsall,

Phil Parkes demonstrates that you've got to be a bit nimble to make the top grade in goal.

looked hard and often at young Parkes before turning elsewhere to sign a goalkeeper.

I admit to being one of those who felt at the time 'they can't all be wrong'. Subsequent events have shown they were.

A good-natured giant of over six feet, Phil is a quiet lad. Rangers, in fact, think he is too quiet on the field – and have worked hard in training to get him to dominate his penalty area and make his presence felt by shouting more often to his own defenders.

Parkes needn't take it to heart. Ten years ago I remember Spurs levelling the very same 'criticism' at the equally modest Pat Jennings.

They have a lot in common, Parkes and Jennings. Physical strength, natural ability and the remarkable knack for big men of dealing so well with ground shots. Both are willing to listen to advice, but have sufficient self-belief to use their own judgement when required.

Parkes made his first positive step to international recognition in the summer of 1972 when he interrupted his honeymoon to understudy Shilton on an England Under-23 tour of East Germany, Poland and Russia.

It was a sacrifice which proved worthwhile, even though Phil was not called upon to play in any of the three games. He impressed manager Sir Alf Ramsey and made Shilton aware of the challenge to come.

'I remember feeling a bit sorry for Phil when he did not get a game,' recalls Shilton, 'but he never complained. I liked his attitude and the way he worked so hard in training.'

The pay-off came for Parkes the following season when Shilton passed the age limit and Phil established himself as number one choice for the Under-23 side.

Indeed, that campaign of 1972–3 was particularly memorable for Parkes. He did not miss a single game as Rangers, in company with Burnley, romped away with promotion from the Second Division.

Last season, when Q.P.R. outshone several of their more fashionable London rivals, Parkes' reputation grew as he adjusted to the demands of the First Division. He took a few games to click into form – but, like the team as a whole, went from strength to strength.

Perhaps the greatest tribute comes from his skipper Terry Venables. 'With each of my three clubs I've had the good fortune to be in the same team as an outstanding goalkeeper. At Chelsea it was Peter Bonetti, at Tottenham it was Pat Jennings. And I rate Phil in the same class,' says Terry.

Above: Oops! Even Phil Parkes has trouble holding the ball. *Below:* Parkes goes up with safe hands to take a high ball.

DAVE CLEMENTS–the Players' Player

Dave Clements, of Everton and Northern Ireland, is no soccer super-star. But I question whether there is a better or more genuine all-purpose footballer in the First Division.

Clements is the kind of player you take for granted. He's been in England for nearly twelve years – and seldom hit the headlines. He's served four different clubs yet his transfer fees have totalled little more than £150,000.

Only in the past year or so, since moving to Everton and taking over the captaincy of the Irish team, has Dave gained the kind of recognition he deserves. I hate to trot out that corny description of a 'players' player' . . . but I've got to admit that it fits Clements like a glove.

The undeniable fact is that Dave is rated more highly by team-mates and First Division opponents than by the fans on the terraces. He is a workmanlike player rather than an eye-catcher.

Perhaps Dave has created his own image by his willingness to fill any position for club or country. His thirty-odd appearances for Northern Ireland include games at full-back, wing-half, inside-forward and orthodox winger. Clements has always been ready to 'fit in' and give 100 per cent.

There are those who believe that if Dave had been allowed to settle as a striker he would have developed into a more glamorous personality. He has certainly proved his match-winning qualities with several spectacular goals for Northern Ireland: probably the most memorable being the decider in the 1–0 victory over the Scots at Windsor Park, Belfast, in 1967.

Clements was a left-winger when, at the age of seventeen, he won an Irish amateur 'cap' with Portadown and was snapped up by Wolves for a few thousand pounds. But he never measured up to expectations at Molineux and was placed on the transfer list.

Jimmy Hill was in charge of Coventry at the time. Jimmy, thwarted by Wolves when he originally tried to sign Dave from Portadown, didn't miss his second chance. And Clements was soon given the chance to prove his first-team worth at Coventry.

It was when Clements took over a defensive role that he really began to blossom out. Although switched around from time to time, to meet Coventry's needs, he starred in the side which gained promotion to the First Division.

But the pendulum swung the other way for Dave after he was transferred to Sheffield Wednesday, along with striker Brian Joicey, in 1971–2. For he suddenly found himself back in the Second Division.

Clements captained the Hillsborough side, but became unsettled when he was continually shuffled from position to position when he wanted to settle in the 'back four'. So he made his feelings known early in 1973–4 and was reluctantly made available for transfer.

It is remarkable, on reflection, that there was no rush for his signature. Dave was on offer for a month before Everton boss Billy Bingham eventually took him to Goodison Park for a relatively modest £70,000.

Bingham, knowing Dave's value from his own spell as Irish team boss, never intended allowing Clements to join any club other than Everton. He just bided his time to clinch the deal at a bargain price.

Clements was Bingham's first buy for Everton, part of a long-term plan to build a championship side. It is an interesting alliance. No Irishman has ever managed a club which has won the First Division title, but Bingham believes he can do it.

And he hopes the versatile Clements will help Everton hit the jackpot . . . and enable his fellow-countryman to make soccer history.

Dave Clements, a capable Irishman, who has played in England for twelve years.

Clements moves into the attack and the West Ham defence is under real pressure.

TOMMY HUTCH-ISON the Entertaining Winger

Tommy Hutchison is one of a handful of players in the First Division who have proved beyond argument that there is a future for natural wingers in English football – providing they are good enough.

To see Scottish international Hutchison in action down the left touchline for Coventry City is to realise why old-timers drool about the delights of orthodox wing play.

He can pick a ball up in his own half of the field and set off on a mazy fifty-yard run, tormenting opposing defenders and upsetting the most carefully-laid pre-match tactical plans.

Hutchison, like every winger of his type since the game began, can also frustrate the fans on occasions by trying to beat too many opponents or even the same one too often. But you can bet your life he will always leave the cash customers with something to talk about.

When playing for Blackpool, Tommy shows he can streak past the Huddersfield defence.

It is this tendency to over-elaborate which caused a number of top clubs to hesitate about paying a £100,000-plus fee for Tommy during four seasons while he was parading his skills with Blackpool. But most of those who turned him down have regretted it ever since Hutchison joined Coventry.

And it wasn't only at club level that Tommy took a long time to win full acknowledgement of his match-winning qualities. Scotland ignored his international claims until 1973. Then their team boss Willie Ormond openly confessed his amazement that the skilful Hutchison had waited so long for his first cap.

Tommy, while ready to concede that he dwells on the ball at times, is philosophical about his career pattern. He got used to disappointment in his teenage days as a juvenile footballer in Fifeshire. 'I was turned away more often than a door-to-door salesman,' he cracks.

Dundee United, Forfar Athletic, Raith Rovers and – down south – Blackburn Rovers and Oldham Athletic all rejected Hutchison after trials. It was finally left to Alloa to show the judgement the others lacked and sign Tommy as a professional.

Alloa obviously know a brilliant youngster when they see one: the same club launched the late and great John White, of Spurs, on the way to stardom.

Next man to play an important part in Hutchison's development was ex-England centre-forward Stan Mortensen, who as boss of Blackpool paid Alloa a fee of around £9,000 for Tommy.

Mortensen was impressed by Hutchison's ball-control and speed for a player who, at nearly six feet, was exceptionally tall for a winger. 'The day I signed Tommy I knew I had a bargain. I'm only surprised it took Scotland so long to give him a chance,' says Stan.

Blackpool bobbed up and down between the First and Second Division during Hutchison's stay at Bloomfield Road. When they were relegated at the end of 1970–1, he became restless for a place in the big league.

But he had to wait more than a year before Blackpool reluctantly made him available for transfer – and Coventry, desperate for more flair up front, agreed to pay the asking price.

Coventry team boss Gordon Milne was the man who backed his opinion with hard cash. I suspect that he saw in Hutchison an outside-left, who even if he doesn't score as many goals as he should, with the rare ability to turn opposing defences inside-out just as Milne's old Liverpool team-mate Peter Thompson had done when they were together at Anfield.

REG DRURY Looks Back to 1939

Who was the England centre-forward who scored four First Division goals in his last Football League game? Try that soccer quiz question on your dad or your grandad . . . if either of them come up with the right answer they are a bit special.

It really happened. Arsenal's famous Ted Drake is the man who finished his League career with a four-timer – against Sunderland at Highbury on Saturday, 2 September 1939.

The date is, of course, the clue to this unique feat. For less than twenty-four hours later, Britain declared war on Germany and the next official Football League matches didn't take place until 31 August 1946.

Drake played regularly during the war, when he was an R.A.F. officer, but by August 1946 a back injury had ended his active career. He became a manager, first with Reading and then with Chelsea – and was in charge at Stamford Bridge in 1954–5 when Chelsea won the League championship for the only time in the club's history.

What else happened, soccer-wise, on the day before war broke out? I turned back the files of the *News of the World* to find out, and it made fascinating reading.

There were far more goals scored, both by teams and individuals, in those days. Bournemouth beat Northampton 10–0 in the Third Division (South) and Newcastle were 8–1 winners against Swansea in the Second Division.

In addition to Drake's four, in Arsenal's 5–2 victory over Sunderland, no fewer than five players claimed hat-tricks.

Two of them were scored in a Second Division match at The Hawthorns where Spurs beat West Bromwich 4–3. Johnny Morrison got three goals for Spurs (two of them in the opening couple of minutes) and West Brom's Eric Jones did likewise but still finished on the losing side.

Only one of the forty-four League fixtures ended in a goalless draw. The teams concerned? Crewe and Hartlepool – so, for them at least, times haven't changed all that much.

My research showed that referees used to get tough thirty-five years ago. Liverpool right-back Alec Harley was sent off at Anfield, and a couple of fans

Ted Drake, one of England's great centre-forwards, finished his League career in 1939 with four goals against Sunderland in September 1939.

who ran on to the pitch to protest had to be removed by the police. But, even with ten men, Liverpool beat Chelsea 1–0 with a goal by Cyril Done.

That season was just three games old when it was ended by the kick-off of the 'Big Match' with Adolf Hitler. So I looked to see who were the success sides at the time.

Blackpool topped the First Division with a maximum six points, followed by Sheffield United and Arsenal with five apiece. Middlesbrough were rock-bottom with a single point, but Leeds and Blackburn were only goal-average above them.

Luton and Birmingham led the Second Division, each with five points. Reading and Exeter were the Third Division (South) pacemakers with five points.

If you are still at school, you probably have never even heard of Accrington Stanley – who were top of the Third Division (North) with three wins and six points. They went out of existence after dropping out of the League thirteen seasons ago.

It is impossible to compare attendances, for the people of Britain had other things than football on their minds on that fateful day in September 1939.

Hitler had invaded Poland and been warned that if he did not withdraw his troops by the following morning, the British and French governments would declare war. Children had been evacuated from the big cities (I know, I was one of them) and the war clouds were gathering ominously.

So soccer crowds were way below average, with 20,000 the highest – at Arsenal, Blackpool, Birmingham and Cardiff. That Cardiff attendance is the most surprising, since the Welsh club were then in the Third Division.

Yet some of the crowds that day were still better than the same clubs attract in 1974. Chester and Rochdale, for instance, both had 6,000 to watch home games. Brentford, admittedly a First Division side, drew 11,000 to Griffin Park.

If I may be permitted a personal recollection, vague though it is through the mists of time, I was among those who went to a match on that afternoon of 2 September 1939.

Having arrived at my new 'home' in Northampton the previous day, a somewhat bewildered ten year old clutching a gas-mask, I went to the County Ground and paid my three old pence to see a reserve game against West Ham.

I remember we kids were allowed to sit on the grass behind one of the goals, and that we got plenty of action for our money – for the score was 5–3.

But I've got to admit I couldn't recall who'd won until I consulted the Combination results in that dusty *News of the World* to find it was Northampton.

Just as well, I suppose, on the day the first team had suffered that ten-goal beating at Bournemouth.

Another typical action picture of Drake. Note the long sleeves and long pants of Arsenal's best scoring centre-forward.

SUPERMAC WAS ONE OF SOCCER'S SUPER BARGAINS

by Terry McNeill

Here's a question to test your football knowledge: What have Malcolm Macdonald, Roger Davies and Ian Hutchinson in common, apart from the obvious fact that they are all strikers?

The answer is they all came into the big-time from non-League football and they are just three examples of how clubs can find a bargain among the part-timers in sections such as the Southern League and the Northern Premier League.

Macdonald's value, if ever Newcastle were tempted to transfer him, must be in the region of £400,000 if you accept that Bob Latchford is rated at £350,000 after his move from Birmingham to Everton last February.

Macdonald has scored far more First Division goals than Latchford, and is also an established international.

And the astonishing thing about him is that he cost Fulham a trifling £1,500 when they signed him from Southern Leaguers Tonbridge, before he went to Luton and then Newcastle.

In those days, he played as many times at full-back as centre-forward, but Harry Haslam, manager of Luton now, saw the possibilities in Supermac, as they call him in the North-East, as a regular goal-scorer.

Harry, who left Tonbridge for Fulham, went back for Macdonald. He was convinced that the young lad languishing with a club unknown outside Kent had what it takes.

Never has a manager's judgement been more vindicated and Supermac's startling success is a superb advertisement for Southern League soccer.

But Macdonald is only one of the growing band who have made their mark from football's backwaters a few years after they thought their chances of recognition at the highest level had vanished.

Chelsea's Hutchinson and Bill Garner were playing against each other in the Southern League five years ago, never dreaming that they would become colleagues in the First Division.

Hutchinson has had a terrible time with injuries since Chelsea took a chance on him, but he has proved his ability with them, and there is not a braver player anywhere.

Hutchinson's fee? A paltry £2,000!

The ref puts an end to a slight confrontation between Arsenal and Leeds players.

Garner, taller and perhaps even more dangerous in the air than Hutchinson, cost Chelsea £85,000 when they obtained him from Southend, but had they bothered to take a look at him with Bedford a few years earlier, they could have saved themselves most of that fee.

Garner, after being discarded by Notts County – he never played in the first team – drifted into minor football with Loughborough United before he tried his luck with Bedford.

Southend saw him score consistently for them, and then took the plunge. And when they sold him they made a profit of more than £70,000.

Davies holds the record for a non-League transfer, £14,000. That was the price Brian Clough, then manager of Derby, paid to Worcester City, and though that's the most ever for a player outside the Football League, it's still pitifully small when you consider what he's worth now.

Bryan King is one of Britain's finest uncapped goalkeepers, and his current value must be more than £100,000. Brilliantly effective for Millwall over the years, this ambitious twenty-seven-year-old was a snip from Wimbledon for £1,000, a shrewd piece of buying by manager Benny Fenton.

King is unfortunate that he belongs to the same era as Peter Shilton, Ray Clemence, Phil Parkes and Alan Stevenson, who are all ahead of him in the England queue, yet he loses little in comparison with these established stars.

And there's a young centre-forward who helped Plymouth into the semi-finals of last season's League

Cup whose valuation has soared with every goal in League football.

Yet Plymouth were once reluctant to sign him for a few hundred pounds from Chorley, the Northern Premier League club. Paul Mariner was recommended to Plymouth and was keen enough to go on trial with them. However Plymouth were not impressed and sent him home.

But again Plymouth were reminded of his potential and this time when he was sent to the West Country he scored goals for them on their pre-season tour. They had second thoughts, and signed him but what a bargain they almost spurned.

Perhaps the most surprising character of all the rich nuggets to come out of obscurity is Tony Book, now Manchester City's manager. Tony was playing for Bath City under the management of Malcolm Allison, and had long before given up hopes of making the grade.

Then Malcolm went to Maine Road as coach, and he quickly sent for the twenty-nine-year-old Book. The result was astounding.

Book went on to play at right-back in three Cup Finals, the F.A. Cup, the League Cup and the European Cup Winners' Cup at an age when many players are thinking about retirement.

Book is the supreme example of a man overlooked for years who had much to offer the First Division.

I wonder how many more jewels there are tucked away in part-time soccer. Perhaps if the big clubs bothered to take a deeper look at minor football, they would save themselves a small fortune later.

Dashing Bryan King, Millwall's goalkeeper, goes into action.

Chelsea's Ian Hutchinson beats Arsenal's John Roberts in a heading duel.

Hutchinson shows himself as a trapeze artist.

FOOTBALL FARMERS by Don Evans

When Liverpool striker and creator Kevin Keegan mentioned that he was thinking of obtaining an old English sheepdog I was able to suggest that if he had a word with Burnley striker Paul Fletcher he might learn something to his advantage.

For Paul and his charming wife had a magnificent bitch from which they had bred a fine litter of sheepdogs. Not only could another litter be on the way, but from Paul and his wife, Kev could also get some first-class advice on how to rear the animal.

At the time the Liverpool striker was thinking of purchasing a cottage in Wales, along with enough acreage to rear animals when and if he so wished. And, thinking of Kev's ambition, I realised just how many animal lovers and indeed breeders there are among our soccer stars.

For instance, if Kevin decided to go in for pig-breeding he need look no further than Anfield, and glance over his shoulder to that redoubtable Liverpool full-back Alec Lindsay. Before leaving Bury for Anfield Alec was a breeder of pigs in a big way and considered quite an authority of the subject.

Indeed, I fully expect him, when his playing days are drawing to a close, to go back into the business. Certainly when we chatted one day at Liverpool we both got rather nostalgic about the country life and our mutual love of all things associated with it, well nearly all.

If, on the other hand, it was cattle that appealed to Kevin Keegan then he would do better popping across Stanley Park and having a word with Everton's Dave Clements.

Back home in Ireland Dave was, before coming across the Channel to join the English League, a farmer and cattle-breeder. Indeed one could say he still is, for he still retains his farm, it being managed in his soccer absence by his father, who also owns a cattle-rearing farm.

I have talked with Dave, in the then truly magnificent country mansion – complete with minstrels' gallery and the rest – which he owned in the Derbyshire hills about cattle-breeding. Believe me, if Alec Lindsay is something of an authority on pigs then the same can be said about Dave and cattle.

Not all that far really from Dave's home – near Chesterfield at that time – before he joined Everton, lived Bill Anderson, the assistant manager of Nottingham Forest who was for so many years the deeply respected manager of Lincoln – and a cattle-owner also.

The difference between Bill and Dave was that while Dave had his own farm, Bill's beasts used to safely graze on the ancient communal land of South Common at Lincoln.

A breeder of a different sort, in that his animals are of a small variety, is Leeds United's Scottish international goalkeeper David Harvey. His particular hobby is the breeding of rabbits, and like the

Alec Lindsay – used to breed pigs.

Kevin Keegan in action against West Ham. Off-field would like to breed animals one day.

other lads I've mentioned, he's a real authority on the subject – and has the prize cards, medals, etc. to prove my point.

Liverpool, Leeds, Lincoln or Ireland, I think you'll get the point, that footballers of today, many of them at least, may be involved in a big-time, glamour, hurly-burly industry, but away from it they really do get back to basics in a commendable way.

I have mentioned but a few of the 'farmer' type of footballers, there are many more. And if we come down to those who love individual animals, dogs in particular, then the list really seems never-ending.

At George Best's digs in Chorlton-cum-Hardy, only a long goal-kick or so from where I live in Manchester, there is a grand old chap, a shaggy Cocker Spaniel of the age of thirteen and the name of Kim.

These days he is blind but you would never know. When I call, remembering me of long acquaintance now, he sniffs hard, possibly scenting my Labrador as well, then gives his tail an almighty thump or two of pleasure.

But let George walk in and the beloved Kim goes into raptures of delight. As his owner, Mrs Mary Fullaway, will tell you 'If George is away for a week-end you have to stand clear when Kim "sees" him back.'

With G.B. having been at Mrs Fullaway's so long the dog and he have grown up together, and it shows in the affection one holds for the other. And, as I say, the list is never-ending.

Everton's David Lawson has a magnificent Setter and, when he first went from Huddersfield to Goodison I was amused, on being introduced to the dog, to hear that in this so partisan soccer city where Liverpool are known as the Reds and Everton as the Blues that the name of David's dog was 'Red'.

Goodison is, by the way, the name of the race-horse owned by former Everton and England centre-half Brian Labone, one of many players or ex-players who own horses.

I don't know whether they are any good at picking winners because of this, but sometimes when I look down from the Press Box and see players capturing stray dogs on the pitch I ponder: 'Well, they all seem to be dog-lovers anyway – and I suppose the dogs know this'.

Paul Fletcher (Burnley) breeds sheepdogs.

SPORTS QUIZ QUESTIONS

Soccer

1. Who were the finalists in last season's League Cup?
2. How much did Denis Law cost Manchester City when they signed him from Manchester United?
3. Derek Dougan played in his first Cup Final in 1960. Who for?
4. What were the results of England's World Cup qualifying matches with Poland in 1973?
5. How many London clubs has Keith Weller played for?
6. Who scored the goal for Bristol City that knocked Leeds out of last season's F.A. Cup?

Table Tennis

1. Where were the first World Championships staged, and when?
2. How many world singles titles did Victor Barna win? When did he win his first title?
3. Name the first English-born player to win a world singles title.
4. Who was the first Asian to win a world championship?
5. Who won the first world title for China, and when?
6. Where was the first Table Tennis Association formed? What was it then called?

Cricket

1. Who was vice-captain of the M.C.C. touring side in the West Indies last winter?
2. How many wickets did Bob Massie take for Australia in the Lord's test against England in 1972?
3. Who has taken over from Brian Taylor as captain of Essex?
4. Name the famous Australian fast-bowler who plays for Leicestershire?
5. Who captained New Zealand in their tour of England last year?
6. Can you name the Sheffield United footballer who plays cricket for Worcestershire?

Angling

1. What is an alevin?
2. What does an elver grow into?
3. Which fish is often called 'the lady of the stream'.
4. Name three sharks most common in British Isles waters.
5. What two sea breams inhabit British waters in most numbers?
6. Where do you find a razorfish in its natural state?

Golf

1. Which American golfer set up a record by winning the first three tournaments and £46,000 in 1974?
2. Who played in Britain's Walker Cup team while still a schoolboy?
3. Who in amateur golf is known as The Duke?
4. Which soccer team plays in an annual golf tournament for a cup presented by its manager?
5. The first player to win two million dollars on the U.S. tour was Trevino, Palmer, Nicklaus or Player?
6. In a round of golf how many miles do you walk – three, four, five or six?

Boxing

1. Only two professional boxers beat Muhammad Ali. Name them.
2. What were the two new weight-divisions created in British boxing in 1973? Who became the first champions at these weights?
3. Joe Bugner fought two former world heavyweight champions. Who were they and what were the results?
4. Who did Ken Buchanan take the world lightweight title from? Who did he lose it to?
5. George Foreman won the world heavyweight title from Joe Frazier in January 1973. How many times did he defend the championship that year and against whom?
6. Name the boxers who won gold medals at the Commonwealth Games in New Zealand in 1974 for England, Northern Ireland, Scotland and Wales.

Swimming

1. Name the British swimmer who retired for the third time after winning a gold medal in the 1974 Commonwealth Games?
2. Where are the next world swimming championships?
3. Who prevented Scotland's David Wilkie from winning a hat-trick of gold medals in the 1974 Commonwealth Games?
4. Who was acclaimed the world's greatest woman swimmer then shocked the world in 1973 by announcing her retirement at seventeen?
5. Who coached Wales to their only swimming gold medal in the 1974 Games?
6. Will there be another British Commonwealth Games?

Follow Through–to the Top
by JOHNNY LEACH
(Twice Champion of the World)

'Keep the head down, eyes on the ball and *FOLLOW-THROUGH!*'

That's sound advice for a player of any ball game in which control and accuracy matter. It is particularly vital in the superspeed sport of table tennis where you are dealing with a light celluloid ball carrying top-, or bottom-spin, and possibly side-spin in addition to pace. To be safe your return must travel low over the 6-inch high net and find a deep target near the baseline.

If you fail to keep your eyes glued on the ball, and neglect to complete a stroke with a follow-through to the full natural extent of the playing arm, the result can only be to your embarrassment. You'll find the ball will land in the net, or go straight on the floor. You might not even manage to hit it at all!

The follow-through is not just an extravagant flourish but an essential part of each stroke which must never be neglected, despite the need for a rapid move of position ready to receive your opponent's return. But don't let this fluster you. Most strokes, correctly performed, will take you naturally into a convenient neutral position of readiness.

Assuming that you are a right-handed player using the orthodox Western 'shake hands' grip and sideways-on stance to play most shots, your most convenient neutral position is a central one at a full arm's length from the table edge.

Nicely balanced on the balls of the feet, knees slightly bent, you are ready for anything. One simple movement forward, backward, or to either side will put you in a position to cope with an opponent's return to any part of your court. And finding this neutral position between strokes isn't difficult with practice. A full follow-through leads you automatically into it.

Take the basic 'push' strokes. These are best made from the appropriate sideways-on-stance, backhand or forehand. Starting with the forearm horizontal and bat blade tilted slightly back at the top, the bat is moved in a forward and slightly downward direction towards the ball. You should be able to almost 'feel' contact being made with the ball. Then, without pause, your movement must be allowed to continue smoothly forward to a natural extent after the ball has left the bat.

During this action the weight of your body shifts from the back to the front foot. At its conclusion all you have to do is to step back into the neutral position ready for the next move.

For the forehand top-spin drive the arm movement normally starts from a position behind the body, the bat being held at about waist height. Contact with the ball should be made when it is just about level with the body, by which time the bat will be a little above waist height. The playing arm is then moved forward and upward, the bat brushing the top of the ball to impart top-spin, then continuing its path.

The full natural extension of the playing arm's follow-through should take the bat to a position at near head height in front of the body. The shoulders, meantime, having started at right-angles to the net, are now almost parallel with it – as required for the neutral position next to be adopted.

The backhand drive is played in a similar manner, except the feet positions are, of course, reversed. Also, contact on the backhand wing is normally made somewhat earlier, and the wrist is often turned to generate extra top-spin. This means that the follow-through is made more across the body with the bat finishing in front of the right shoulder.

Since most players tend to favour forehand as

Johnny Leach – considered to be the finest judge of the game.

opposed to backhand it has become customary to adopt a modified sideways-on stance for the backhand drive. Taking up a position at an angle of 45 degrees with the end of the table, a player will make his shot towards the front of his body. At the same time he pivots at the hips to assist the transfer of body weight from left to right foot.

This modification is quite acceptable, providing compensation is made by exaggerating the follow-through. This permits the bat to stay in contact with the ball for the maximum possible time, and helps to make up for loss of power, control and accuracy.

The heavily accentuated top-spin drive known as the Loop is the one with the most spectacular follow-through. For the high loop, which causes the ball to lift high over the net, bounce and then kick violently from the table surface, it is necessary to brush the back of the ball very severely.

The bat, therefore, is brought vertically upward and, after brushing the ball, it continues its upward path to finish high above the player's head. For the low loop, the result of which is less spin but greater speed, a larger area of ball is brushed on contact and the path taken by the bat is more forward than upward.

The approach for defensive back-spin strokes is made with the bat at shoulder height, and one aims to make contact at about waist height when the ball is dropping. Knees and trunk should bend as the arm movement progresses in a chopping motion forward and downward. The desired point of contact is behind and below the centre of the ball.

The bat is then allowed to follow-through in an upward curve, finishing at near shoulder height if a sandwich bat is being used. With an ordinary, pimpled rubber bat the chopping movement should be more directly downward on the ball so the follow-through ends at about knee height.

Forehand and backhand chop strokes are made in a similar manner, but the backhand differs slightly in its follow-through. The length of the latter is naturally determined by the intervention of the elbow joint. This is an advantage, because to follow-through too far in this instance would introduce undesirable side-spin.

Such is the speed of modern championship play that some aspects of textbook stroke play must necessarily be modified. For example, the ideal position from which to play all strokes I have described here is from a full sideways-on stance, yet frequently you will see top international stars play these strokes satisfactorily from a position almost square-on to the table. How do they get away with it?

Well, it *is* a question of 'getting away with it' because modifications of the ideal method must inevitably mean a loss of power, and less margin for error. Your modern champions will compensate in

Bobby Butlin and Johnny Leach line up with David Newman and Belinda Chamberlain, chosen as Boy and Girl of the Year in the annual award organized by Butlin's Holiday Camps and the News of the World.

The Johnny Leach grip.

some way for every liberty he takes with the textbook. He will compensate for lack of backswing, and lack of body assistance to a stroke by pivoting from the hips to simulate a sideways-on movement.

However unorthodox his stroke may be at its start, you may be sure it will be right at the finish. In fact he will exaggerate the vitally important follow-through movement, which is the proof of the whole stroke.

I hope I have demonstrated the importance of the follow-through from a technical point of view, but the expression has special significance today in a broader context. For several years Britain has had to take a back seat in both World and European table tennis championships.

Yet those years have not been wasted. They have been spent wisely in the encouragement of talented young players through such far-sighted competitions as the *News of the World* National Coaching Scheme at Butlins Holiday Camps, complemented by the now wide-ranging activities of the official associations whose talent-spotting net virtually guarantees that no young player of special promise will be allowed to slip through.

Gradually, standards are improving. We are catching up the likes of China, Japan, Russia and Sweden. There is good reason to believe that when the 1977 World Championships are staged in England our leading players will be ready to challenge strongly for the main titles. But this can only happen if the players follow through by their own efforts the careful coaching given to them at the start of their careers.

The talent you show as a beginner may win you numerous minor awards, but you are squandering that talent if you are not prepared to work at it and improve it to the maximum. Alas, for every hundred promising juniors I spot every year, usually only one follows through to top senior class, let alone top world class.

One can understand why so many potential champions fall by the wayside. The climb to the top is long and arduous, and modern life has so many diversions to offer which are more attractive than training. But regular training and practice is the only way to gain consistent success. If you want to be a champion you've got to work hard for it. Is success worth all the sacrifices you are called to make? Anyone who has made the grade will tell you: YES!

CRICKET MUST ENCOURAGE YOUNG ENGLISH TALENT

by Peter Smith

It is time to turn round to the overseas born cricketer and say: 'Thanks very much for coming. We've enjoyed your stay. But we must learn to get along without you now.'

English cricket MUST start standing on it's own feet if it is going to retain the tremendous interest it has generated over the last four or five years.

Ever since Ray Illingworth emerged victorious from the fight for the Ashes in Australia during the winter of 1970–1, the game has gone from strength to strength. Cricket authorities have been accused, quite rightly at times, of moving too slowly and missing out on numerous opportunities.

Not after that series victory in Australia. They got down to some tough bargaining resulting in thousands of pounds being poured into the game from sponsorship and other means giving each county a chance to get out of the red and into the black.

That money will only continue to come into the game as long as the public interest is there. The public will only stay interested as long as the England side prove they are worth supporting on the international scene.

And that means breeding the type of player to hold his own in the tough and demanding world of Test cricket. Not only breeding him which is a slow and agonising process but offering him the opportunity to show his qualifications once he has gone through his apprenticeship.

Too many youngsters are finding there is little light at the end of that apprenticeship road, the way ahead blocked by county sides going out to sign ready-made players from abroad in their impatience to win one of the four major trophies now up for the taking each season.

This is why I believe the time has come to restrict the entry of overseas born players into English cricket whatever their worth as match winners and their potential as crowd pullers. We must not depend on other countries producing such players but make every effort possible in producing our own.

Nobody has taken more delight than myself in watching Barry Richards move effortlessly from nought to three figures playing for Hampshire, accelerating with the grace and smoothness of a tried and tested racing car leaping into the lead of a Grand Prix race from the starting grid.

Richards at his best is sheer magic. There is nobody else in English cricket to touch him. Any more than there is anybody to match the athleticism of Clive Lloyd swooping in the field for Lancashire or Rohan Kanhai and Alvin Kallicharran tearing apart opposing attacks when they are batting in harness for Warwickshire.

There are many others born overseas whose loss to the county cricket scene will be sadly felt. But it is

Rohan Kanhai puts one away while wicket-keeper Alan Knott looks on.

Ray Illingworth, England's former skipper, hits out at Australian bowling in Test Match.

worth losing them if the future of England at Test level is going to look more secure.

I am not suggesting that such players should be banned overnight, never to darken the shore of England again unless on Test duty for their respective countries. The change-over can be a gradual process.

All overseas players in county cricket not qualified to play for England should be allowed to continue until their present contracts expire. This would make sure they helped to keep the game alive and attractive until the locally born player had developed sufficiently to take over.

At the same time I would like to hear the Test and County Cricket Board announce now that no overseas born players not eligible to play for England would be registered if it meant that a county had more than one on the staff.

That, in the future, should be the absolute limit. Just one overseas born player per county. Today some county sides are capable of fielding five or six overseas born players. It is a short-sighted policy. The county sides concerned cannot possibly prosper in the long run. The inclusion of star overseas players is a costly business and no guarantee of success.

Far too many of the overseas born players are no better than English players if only the county organisations took the trouble to scout around. They are taken on because a county side has seen a shortage in their side and grabbed at the first person they have found to provide them with temporary cover.

I know one overseas born player who was signed on after being watched deliver just a few balls in a hastily arranged net in a public park! Others engaged on the evidence of three or four performances for the county second team. Once engaged, the county has been forced to play them in the first team in an attempt to justify the wages being paid.

Rohan Kanhai goes down to make a delightful square cut.

I know that many years ago boys at school had no alternative but to play soccer in the winter – or rugby – and criket in the summer. Today the education authoritiecs otter them the opportunity to play many other sports, most of them easier to organise than a cricket match and requiring less in the way of facilities.

Yet I cannot believe there is as great a shortage of talent around as many people claim. The talent must be there among fourteen, fifteen and sixteen year olds if the county clubs organised a scouting system to find it in a way football clubs swoop on school and park sides looking for their star soccer players of tomorrow.

Left: **Ray Illingworth in action against West Indies. Alvin Kallicharran enjoys putting this one away. Barry Richards, sheer magic when at his best. Clive Lloyd livens up any game when he gets going.**

Too many county organisations have been content to sit back and wait for schoolboys to approach them instead of detailing their own search parties. Gradually the message is getting home.

Glamorgan have taken a lead by their decision twelve months ago not to re-engage West Indies opening batsman Roy Fredericks because they wanted to give their younger players a start. Others, Kent, Leicestershire, Surrey and Gloucestershire among them, have good links with schools organisations inside their borders.

Yorkshire, too, must be praised for sticking to their policy of engaging Yorkshiremen only. During the transition period when the old side of Brian Close began to break up and the new team was assembled, Yorkshire might easily have panicked and signed an overseas player to ease their shortage. They stayed calm and will benefit in the long run.

I hope other county organisations will now fall in step. They have got to if England is to remain strong internationally. And only a winning England side can ensure that cricket at a lower level continues to prosper.

HOW TO SPIN WITH A FIXED SPOOL REEL

by Brian Harris

Young anglers of today take the fixed-spool reel very much for granted. Yet when I was a lad learning the art of catching fish, I had to use centrepin reels until I was fourteen, when I was given one of the forerunners of the true fixed-spool reel.

It worked on the same principle as the modern fixed-spool reel, in that the line streamed off the front of the spool. This faced up the rod, rather than coming off a spinning drum, as with a free-running centrepin reel.

There the similarity ended. The line had to be removed from a hooked device so that a cast could be made, and it had to be put back into the hook before turning the handle, so that the line could be wound back on to the spool.

And the spool itself revolved, the hook device moving forwards and backwards to spread the line evenly on the spool.

This meant that after about a dozen casts you had to stop fishing and remove the kinks in the line which had been put there by the act of casting it from the stationary spool's front lip, then winding it back with the spool going round.

If you hooked a big fish you were in trouble, since the reel, called the Allcock-Stanley casting reel, was effective only with thin and delicate line – 4-lb test was about the maximum. If the battle was prolonged the line would get into terrible kinks and sometimes snag on a rod-ring and snap.

There were one or two true fixed-spool reels about when I was in my early teens, but they were too expensive for my pocket. The true fixed-spool reel of today, which you can buy for £2.50, has its spool stationary. The line is automatically picked up after casting by a bale-arm, which is activated by winding the reel handle forward about half a turn.

The bale-arm collects the loose line. Then it slips back into a line-roller, which may revolve in the best-designed reels. Or it may be simply of hard metal to resist wear, and the whole bale and its line-roller is wound by the handle around the reel frame at a right-angle to the rod, and it winds the line on to the spool.

This system avoids the kinks put in when the spool itself rotates.

The modern fixed-spool reel also has a built-in braking system or drag, adjustable either by turning a knob on the front of the spool, or by a knob at the rear of the reel body.

This is adjusted so that, with the rod bent in a quarter circle line is just given by the reel drag. The drag is then let off just a fraction, and you know that, short of a fast hard jerk, the fish you hook cannot break your line.

Once you have the big fish on, and the reel yields line with the rod curved round nearly a quarter circle (about an angle of 75 degrees between the butt of the rod and the extremity of the tip) you can add to the resistance of your drag.

This stops the fish getting into a weed-bed or some other snag. For example you can drop the fore-finger of your rod hand on to the lip of the spool and putting on pressure.

This is an effective move since you can add pressure or remove it instantly, and manual braking of the spool is far more delicate than that of the pre-set drag.

Stuart Harris, the writer's son at the age of nine. He caught this 20-lb salmon, spinning with a small bar-spoon.

Grey mullet from a southern estuary taken on light spinning tackle.

Right! Now let's go fishing. Originally, fixed-spool reels were designed for one main purpose. To permit very light spinning baits to be cast long distances on lines of between 2-lb and 8-lb test. The quarry in mind are trout and sea trout, salmon and, to a lesser degree, perch and pike.

In particular, anglers want to be able to cast these light and tiny lures, mainly devon minnows and quill minnows and wagtails, upstream in low, clear water, then wind them rapidly back – faster than the speed of the current, of course.

That tactic, in summer, is effective for salmon, trout and sea trout.

Now the reel is used not only for spinning for predatory fish, but for float and leger fishing as well. But it is in spinning, in the sea as well as in freshwater, that the reel comes into its own and we can enjoy great sport.

In the rivers, streams and canals and lakes we can catch pike, perch, chub, salmon, sea trout and trout, though salmon, sea trout and trout are found only in some clean swift rivers.

In the sea, casting from beaches, rocks, groynes, piers and harbour walls will bring bass, mackerel, garfish, pollack, small coalfish, ballan wrasse. Less frequently you will find cod, flounders, plaice and thick-lipped grey mullet.

Basically, you will need two rods to cover all the types of spinning for the fish I have mentioned. The

Box swivels, large and small. Safe because burred-over ends are visible.

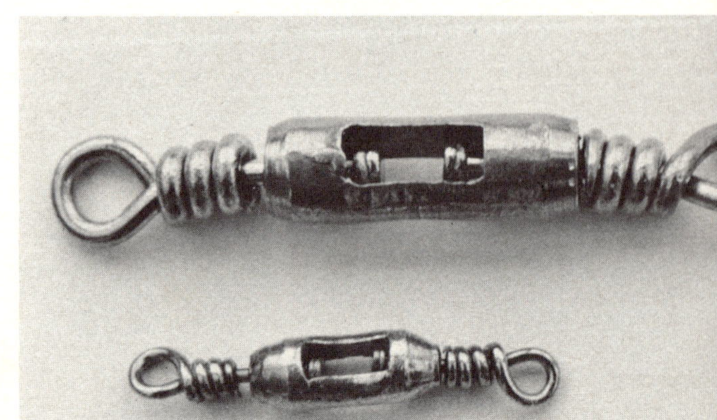

Dangerous country, but fine spinning ground for pollack, mackerel, garfish and ballan wrasse.

first a hollow glass-fibre spinning rod, for lines of 3-lb to 5-lb test, between 7 and $8\frac{1}{2}$ feet in length, and weighing no more than 5 ounces. The second a carp or salmon or pike spinning rod, for lines of 6-lb to 10-lb test, between 9 and 10 feet in length and weighing no more than 12 ounces.

The reel should have a spare spool with it. Try to buy one with a corrosion-resistant finish, since salt-water can ruin a reel quickly if you neglect it. On one spool have, say, 4-lb test line, and on the other, say, 9-lb test.

Fill both spools with line to within approximately $\frac{1}{2}$ inch of the top of the front lip because if you don't you will not be able to cast properly. You can wind the line on first. If it fails to fill, wind on some old wool, thin string or whatever, until the correct level is reached. Then remove the wool, and the line. Rewind the wool on first, then the line.

The light rod is for the following species: perch, chub, trout, sea trout (small ones), bass (small ones), mackerel, garfish, flounders, plaice, grey mullet and small coalfish.

The heavier rod and the spool of stronger line will cope with pike, salmon and big sea trout, big bass, pollack, ballan wrasse and cod up to about 10 lb.

We have rods and a reel with lines. Now we need our spinners, etc. I'd suggest you start by bearing in mind what you will fish for mainly. You may decide only to go for the smaller fish. If so, you only need the light rod and one spool on the reel. It is not much use buying the lures I am going to suggest for salmon if you cannot ever imagine yourself being able to fish in a salmon river!

Here we go: For trout, sea trout, perch, chub, salmon, grey mullet, flounders and plaice – bar-spoons, all gold, all silver, red/silver and red/gold, sizes from half an inch up to $1\frac{1}{4}$ inches in spoon size, plus some up to 2 inches spoon length for pike.

For salmon, sea trout and trout – devon minnows, both metal- and wooden-bodied types, or of plastic, metal from $\frac{3}{4}$ inch to 2 inches, wooden or plastic from 2 inches to 3 inches. Colours: silver-blue, brown-gold, and (for wooden or plastic minnows in size 2 to 3 inches only), 'yellow belly', which is a pale yellow on one side, dark green on the other.

About ten bar-spoons and twenty devon minnows should meet all requirements. You can buy the devon minnow bodies cheaply unfinished and paint them yourself.

For mackerel, bass, garfish, pollack and coalfish – Toby spoons in silver finish and silver/red, Condor spoons about 3 and 4 inches in length (sometimes sold under the name 'German Sprat') and Red Gill plastic sand-eels, the large size only, in silver/green and red/gold finish. The Toby spoons should be $\frac{5}{8}$- and $\frac{7}{8}$-ounce sizes.

In all cases when using the above lures, it is best to tie between traces and line an open box swivel (for salmon a ball-bearing swivel) about size 12 for fish up to 10 lb. Use size 8 for salmon- and pike-size specimens to help prevent the spinning lure passing on twists to kink your line.

The Condor spoon and the plastic sand-eels will not kink the line since they do not spin but wobble or waver and flash. To the free eye of the swivel tie about 2 feet of suitable nylon, and then your lure. But for pike, you need a wire trace of about 10 inches in length because pike tend to cut the nylon trace with their teeth.

Imagine we are going trout spinning in May on a sunny day with the river or stream running fast but clear. Trout, and other fish in rivers, usually face

A pike comes to the boat and still has spirit to fight.

upstream, except in spots where the current eddies and where they may lie facing a current that is circling upstream.

So, you need to walk upstream. The light rod and line is called for, and the lure may be a $\frac{3}{4}$-inch blue/silver devon minnow, or a bar-spoon of your choice with a half-inch spoon length.

You make a cast, flipping the lure some 15 yards upstream and across, and immediately the lure hits water you wind the handle, the pick-up closes, and you wind in line, quite quickly.

It may take several casts before you get the recovery speed right; and expect to catch the bottom a few times before you do. Keep the rod pointing across, slightly upstream, the tip held about a foot above the water, as you wind in.

Sooner or later you will feel a pull and suddenly the rod bends and you have a trout or sea trout pulling hard as the line buzzes from the spool of your reel, perhaps leaping a number of times before you eventually tire your quarry and guide it over the landing-net to be lifted out.

You may need to change lure colour or size, or even type before you catch that first fish.

Similar tactics are used to catch salmon in the summer months when the water is clear and low. A one-inch lure on 6 lb will often suffice, although up to 2 inches can be tried.

For salmon in the cold part of the season – February to the middle of April – the tactics and tackle are different. The idea at this time, with the salmon big, not very lively, and with the rivers running high and strongly, is to fish the flashy spinning lure slowly across the river, within a foot of the river-bed.

To do this a devon minnow of about 3 inches is chosen – whatever colour you fancy, though the yellow belly version is good, preferably plastic or wood.

Tie a ball-bearing swivel to the end of your reel line (10-lb test at least). Add a yard or so of similar nylon, threading on to it the hollow body of your devon. Now slip a red bead on the line and tie on a size 6 or 4 treble hook. The devon rests on the bead and when the current plays on the spinning vanes set near the front the body spins, swivelling on the bead.

You need a lead-weight to get the devon down in the current, and you can attach it on the rod side of the ball-bearing swivel, either by a clip through the swivel eye or by squeezing a lead foldover pattern on the line.

Fighting a big salmon in spring and heavy water is quite a skilful task, but a boy can do it. See the photograph of my own son with a 20-pounder he caught unaided when only nine. He complained of aching arms after a forty-minute battle which included running up and down the bank to keep in touch with the salmon!

Spinning for pike is slightly different. You'll need the heavy rod and line of about 9-lb test. Lures can

This is how the fixed-spool reel is used to fish a Devon minnow. No winding, just a drift round.

Finger pressure on the spool can be delicate.

be the larger bar-spoons, although a 3-inch devon minnow of wood or plastic is a good pike lure. Don't forget to use a short trace of wire. About 10-lb test wire will do.

Pike spinning requires a slow recovery of the spinner, close to the bottom in winter, higher and a bit faster in the summer, where pike fishing is legal in the summer, that is.

Cast alongside weeds and reed-beds, into bays and beside sunken logs. In lakes try the banks where there is deep water close in. When you feel the pike take hold of the lure, pull the hooks home firmly: pike have bony jaws.

Spinning in the sea is done in exactly the same way, in general, as in freshwater. For bass, use the heavier rod and line for most of your fishing, with a Toby spoon or Red Gill. Rocky breakwaters, estuaries, piers, even some open beaches with deep water are the places to try.

Just cast out as far as you can and reel in quite quickly. The same technique works with mackerel and garfish, except that you may use the lighter outfit and have more fun. The Condor spoon, which is narrow and heavy for its size, casts long distances and is specially effective for mackerel and garfish.

When in the West Country (Devon and Cornwall and parts of neighbouring counties, as well as the west and south-west of Ireland) fishing from rocky ledges with deep rock-strewn and weedy water, can produce good pollack to about 8 lb, as well as big ballan wrasse.

The heavy outfit is needed and the best lure (for pollack and ballan wrasse) is the Red Gill sand-eel. With about an ounce of lead above the normal swivel, cast as far as you can, sometimes along the shoreline, and let the lure sink till it's almost on the rocks, then recover line slowly, giving the rod tip an occasional jerk.

You may feel taps as you wind; most likely a pollack is following and nipping at the wriggling tail of your sand-eel. Just keep winding. Then you will feel a terrific pull and the pollack will dive strongly for the rock and weed on the bottom. Don't let the fish get down too far or you'll lose it. This first dive of a good pollack is one of the best things in British sea angling.

Wrasse may occasionally take, intermittently with pollack. They, too, are hard fighters, and many people think they will only take worm and shellfish baits. The Red Gill gets them, though.

Finally, the sea flatfish, flounders and plaice, and the grey mullet. The two flatfish live on the sea-bed so that is where you must fish. You can use either of the two outfits, but in quiet water with a depth of under 20 feet the lighter will give more sport.

Remove the hook from a 2-inch bar-spoon, preferably a silver one, and tie in its place a size 2 long-shank hook on a 6-inch length of 10-lb nylon. Bait

A fine rocky stance in South Wales with deep water close in. Bass are main quarry.

the hook with lugworm, ragworms, a razorfish or a thin strip cut from a squid, about 2 inches long by a ¼ inch wide.

Having cast, let your spoon sink to the sand or mud, then reel in slowly, with pauses of a couple of seconds every two yards or so. You should just feel the spinner vibrating, and the occasional touch on the bottom. Both flounders and plaice will follow the trail of sand and mud the whirling spoon kicks up, then find the baited hook and grab it.

In some estuaries, grey mullet can be taken on a tiny light bar-spoon (spoon length half to three-quarters of an inch) specially with a couple of red ragworms on the treble hook. Cast lightly where the mullet are seen swimming and swirling on the surface, and wind in fairly slowly, keeping the rod high and the spoon just below the surface.

Fixed-spool spinning can give you a terrific range of species and places in your angling. And in general, you don't have to go looking for, or buying bait.

A pike lies on the grass, ready to go back alive, or make a succulent meal for the angler's family.

Jack Nicklaus has Turned GOLF into GOLD

by JACK WOOD

Jack Nicklaus, already the winner of more major titles than any golfer in the game's history and of more cash than Arnold Palmer, the man who did the pace-setting in golf's great gold rush, now aims to have a Nicklaus-designed course in every golfing country.

The target appears an impossible one, but Nicklaus has accepted such challenges before and made it. Without doubt the company structure he has developed is the most complex ever assembled by an individual sportsman.

Golf gives, in my view, a greater chance to amass fame and fortune over an extended period than any other sport. Racing drivers retire in their early or mid-thirties if they are fortunate to survive that long.

Boxers with the odd exception like Ray Robinson and Archie Moore are forced to quit when still young men, and the increasing pressures bring retirement much earlier than in the old days to our footballers.

From an earnings point of view on the course and the chance to exploit his name in other sectors of the game, the golfer has it made in a way which can never be the lot of the others.

In order to achieve his own wide ambitions and identify himself universally with the sport that has given him so much in return for all that he has given to golf, the blond American has set up a number of corporations of which he is the head.

The point being made is that any Mrs Worthington with ambitions for young Johnny should have a look at the golf stage before considering other sports. The gold in golf is being dug at an increasing rate while the rewards in other sports in no way keep pace.

Jack Nicklaus Incorporated embraces course design, ownership, maintenance, clothes and club design. In addition, he is responsible for staging tournaments. One of his companies, John Montgomery Executive Sports, last year ran eleven of the forty-four which go to make up the nine million dollar U.S. tour.

Jack found himself in the unique position of winning the first Ohio Kings Island Open, one heck of a mouthful in any language but the first happening of it's kind since the Dutch, or was it the Scots started knocking something akin to a ball around and finally into a hole some 500 years ago.

The Kings Island course was designed by Nicklaus. The tournament won its place in an already crowded programme via his representations, and his companies own the place. And at the end of four days the first prize of £12,000 was taken by your man himself.

His principal partner Putman Pierman is a thirty-

Tom Weiskopf, along with Lee Trevino, shares No. 2 listing to Jack Nicklaus.

Johnny Miller shows determination before winning the 1973 U.S. Open at Oakmont, Pa. He has just set up a record 63 for the course.

eight-year-old Columbus businessman who has a finger in almost every Nicklaus pie, although the inspiration of a world wide set-up is still the wonderful golf of Big Daddy Jack himself.

His 1973 winnings of 308,000 dollars were a record, and with his victory in the Disney Classic he took his career total to 2,012,000 dollars, thus becoming the first man to pass the 2,000,000 dollar mark.

Discussing the explosion in his fortune and interests, Nicklaus remains modestly objective, insisting that the main purpose of his being is still the winning of golf tournaments.

'My late father set me on the course which has proved such a rewarding and enjoyable one when I was a kid needing sawn-down clubs. Since then few people could have had a fuller or better life. I hate being pompous, getting values overstated, but golf really is a wonderful game and good for all who play it.

'Apart from the physical benefits, and there must be millions all over the world who get exercise they would not otherwise have because they play the game, there is the relaxation the game brings.

'I have designed courses in Japan, the Middle East and Europe. As the game spreads I want to expand the interests of our group. We are serious-minded in business with specialists in every field. But we like to also have fun.'

I have been at the receiving end of his hospitality in the U.S., on his island hideout Great Harbor Cay in the Bahamas and can testify to his generosity, and when in the mood for an evening out, capacity.

He plays in fewer tournaments than any of the other top men but because he sets his sights on the big ones and gives himself plenty of time for a thorough preparation he is the most successful. Now with him in Columbus is his regular caddy when in Britain Jimmy Dickenson.

Jimmy is said to be earning something like £10,000 a year as a member of the Kings Island club staff but will come to this country with the boss when duty like the Open championship calls.

Big Jack has a love–hate relationship with the game. It is said that, Ben Hogan apart, no other player living knows as much about the technique of the game and its application. There may be teachers with a deeper knowledge of theory but it is Nicklaus who converts learning into immense loot.

I have talked of him and his ambitions in detail because he is possibly the most talented, aggressively successful yet most modest sportsman around today. And when the hate bit comes through in his involvement with golf he shoots off to sea where he is a fine fisherman or into the hills to hunt.

Pierman has also gone into golf management but Nicklaus insists that this is a side of the game he must leave alone until he retires. Judging by his first two signings Mr Pierman intends this side of his business to be on the same scale as those in which he and Nicklaus are involved.

Tom Weiskopf was British and Canadian Open champion when he threw in his lot with the organisation and may be only Lee Trevino could argue that Weiskopf is second to only the king himself. The second star in a slowly developing but classic stable is Ben Crenshaw, who gave up a Walker Cup team chance to turn pro and won the first tour event in which he played.

Johnny Miller can assuredly be said to have arrived having won a U.S. Open, Lanny Wadkinsis a fairway gambler with the flair of the superstar, but many consider twenty-two-year-old Crenshaw the heir apparent. Not that the king is thinking of stepping down for a while.

Nicklaus is reputed to have a personal fortune of 20,000,000 dollars. Compared with that sort of cash Britain's Tony Jacklin is in the minor league, but not exactly on the bread-line following his decision to forsake the American tour for the more leisurely pastures of Britain and Europe.

It's fun time at Troon. Lee Trevino kisses the ball after sinking a wonder putt. Lee remains golf's greatest showman.

JOHN CONTEH - He's Pretty and Good by Frank Butler

Who wants to be a millionaire? John Conteh, holder of the European, British and Commonwealth light-heavyweight championships, is completely honest. He does!

Conteh, the handsome athlete born in Liverpool twenty-two years ago, loves the good things that boxing has given him. His dad came to England from Sierra Leone over thirty years ago.

Conteh senior worked hard all his life as a welder to feed and keep his large family . . . he had eight sons and two daughters. In fact, with his wife, Mr Conteh could boast of a football team, including the substitute!

Cash had to be short with such a large family. But they were all happy kids and with John admitting that his staple meals consisted of fish and chips, and stews it's a tribute to those very English dishes that he grew into a six-feet tall lad and one of the hardest hitting light-heavyweights in Europe.

Liverpool is one of the great fight towns in Britain. So it wasn't surprising that John Conteh as a lad drifted into the gymnasium and was soon making quite an impression with the locals.

The experts soon spotted a natural talent. He was fast of foot and had a good left jab. He was, in fact, good at all sports at school. Loved soccer and set up a high-jump record. He also excelled with the javelin and was one of the school's best swimmers.

But boxing was his favourite sport and his hero was, of course, Muhammad Ali or Cassius Clay as Ali was known when Conteh was a twelve-year-old schoolboy.

It's incredible but Conteh was only eight years old when Clay became Olympic light-heavyweight champion in Rome in 1960. John was only twelve when Cassius Clay shook boxing fans by winning the world heavyweight championship from the much-feared Sonny Liston. Clay was only twenty-two at the time.

Conteh moved into an amateur club at Liverpool and tried to style himself on the great Clay. He was successful and as he grew from boyhood to manhood he won forty-six of fifty amateur bouts. He won the A.B.A. middleweight title and the Commonwealth Games gold medal at Edinburgh in 1970.

Though he failed to win a European title, professional fight managers were chasing him for his signature on a contract. George Francis, a former fruit porter in Covent Garden market, worked hardest and offered him £10,000 to sign a contract with him.

Conteh agreed to accept the money on the instalment system and was launched on the professional circuit in 1971. Between October and December of that year John chalked up five easy wins against moderate opposition.

He impressed all the boxing critics and the following year won ten of eleven fights. The opposition wasn't great but as he was only twenty-one it was a good record and he was soon emerging as the best young British boxer and was reckoned to be a better prospect than heavyweight Joe Bugner.

His one defeat at Wembley that year was to drop a points decision to an experienced American named Eddie Duncan. Though it was obviously a set-back, it didn't worry him unduly.

John remained undefeated throughout 1973 which was his best year so far. After outpointing a moderate fighter named Dave Mathews he was taken off to Las Vegas along with Joe Bugner.

Jarvis Astaire, Mister Big of British boxing, had arranged for Bugner to meet Muhammad Ali in the great gambling city of Nevada and also offered John a fight with Terry Daniels, an American heavyweight whose only claim to fame was that he had been knocked out by Joe Frazier in a world heavyweight championship fight.

At this time Conteh's advisers were trying to build him up into a heavyweight and they worked it out

Handsome John has a little of the Muhammad Ali profile.

that a win over Daniels would help boost John's claims in the higher division.

The Liverpool fighter easily stopped the fading Daniels in six rounds but it was decided that though he was tall he was built on greyhound lines and that he wasn't likely to grow into a natural heavyweight and that he would after all concentrate on the light-heavyweight division.

So he returned to England and was steered into a European light-heavyweight championship match against the German Rudi Schmidtke, who had taken this title from British champion Chris Finnegan.

Conteh was not, of course, British champion but he was backed by boxing folk with a lot of influence and the German was offered sufficient money to tempt him to England to defend his newly-won title.

Conteh boxed brilliantly against the German who though not a big puncher, is an aggressive and efficient fighter. John stopped Schmidtke in twelve rounds to become European champion at twenty-one.

The natural box-office fight after this was for him to meet Chris Finnegan for the British and Commonwealth titles for though Schmidtke had taken Finnegan's European crown, it had been agreed all round that Chris had been matched too quickly with the German after a really hard battle against Bob Foster for the world title.

Finnegan and Conteh put up a great fight which ended with the Liverpool boy taking a narrow decision though at one time Finnegan rallied and it looked as though he might have surprised John.

Conteh finished up 1973 with wins over Vicente Rondon, a former world champion, Baby Boy Rolle and Fred Lewis. His one ambition now is, of course, to become world champion but wisely his backers have kept him away from the veteran light-heavyweight champion Bob Foster who gave Finnegan such a bad beating.

Though past his best, Foster is a terrific puncher and the men behind Conteh believe it is better to allow him to grow even older so that the British champion can take him in the twilight of his career.

John Conteh, like his hero Muhammad Ali, is pretty. He's the best-looking boxer in Britain today and is adored by the kids in Liverpool. He already has a Fan Club, nearly 1,000 strong.

He's still a bachelor though he has had to show some of the tricks of Houdini to escape from the dolly girls who simply adore him. He has never forgotten what he owes to his parents and when he got into the big money moved his mum from her council house in Kirby to a £25,000 house in Southport.

His target is to follow in the footsteps of Freddie Mills, the last British boxer to win the world light-heavyweight championship. His task won't be easy but it's an ambition well worth having.

Conteh holds off an onslaught by Canada's Bill Drover but misses with his left as he counters.

It's the Lonsdale Belt
and it's all mine!

We Must Get Our Swimming Priorities Right by BOB DONN

Get your priorities right. Money is not everything. How often have those two phrases been flashed at you – at home, at school and at work?

Well, today, those phrases are being hammered back at their elders by a group of dedicated young sportsmen and women. In this case it is England's swimmers.

Why are they annoyed? Who are they advising to think again about priorities and money? Well, it's the Amateur Swimming Association, the ruling body of swimming in England.

Over the years I have told you how Britain lags behind the world's major swimming countries in preparing for competitive swimming. How, in fact, a tiny country like East Germany, with only a fraction of the population and resources of the world's giants, America and Russia, is now on the pathway to becoming the world's mightiest swimming nation.

Why then does Britain lag behind? It's not lack of money. In the past it has been a lack of dedication. It is not a lack of coaching know-how. So, you may well ask, where is the fault.

Curiously, the problem with English swimming is partly bound up in that so terribly English phrase: 'True Blue Amateurism.' The attitude of the A.S.A. over the years has always been that their main duty is to encourage the teaching of swimming throughout the country and that the competitive disciplines of the sport should take second place to this purpose in life.

Coaches and swimming writers have argued for years that the route to a powerful swimming association is through the shop-window of the sport – competitive swimming.

Nothing encourages young people to adopt a sport more than the gold medal successes of their own country people. This success and the dreams of world-wide travel has transformed the most mundane sports from the fringe of bankruptcy into crowd-attracting spectacles.

This was a lesson Scotland took to heart when they planned their first professional preparation of a swimming team prior to the 1970 Commonwealth Games in Edinburgh. It was a mood nurtured by their National coach John Hogg as he began long-term planning for the Commonwealth Games in Christchurch in 1974. It's history now that a young and largely inexperienced Scottish side while winning fewer medals than England created a greater overall impression.

They did not have a motto for the New Zealand Games but Virgil's words seem appropriate: 'Success nourished them; they seemed to be able, and so they were able.'

This success was nourished because they got their priorities right and were backed by a swimming association with little money in the kitty but said to the swimmers: 'Money is not everything. You get on with your training and let us worry about the money.'

By sharp contrast England, despite having no money worries, did not have the same approach to competition. Their training camps were not so frequent. Team atmosphere was sluggish in being developed. Kim Wickham, an eighteen year old from Darlington who swims for Scotland because her father was born in Edinburgh said: 'The Scottish training camps are clannish . . . and I like that because it creates a tremendous feeling. You realise you are letting the team down with a poor swim.'

Unfortunately, Scotland's example as a leader made little impression on the British selectors, a body controlled by the Amateur Swimming Association. The European Championships were staged in Vienna in August with the East Germans confirming their world status. But the lessons of the Christchurch Games was lost in the petty squabbling of officials who are still trying to formulate a British Swimming Federation, a fifteen-year-old discussion between England, Wales and Scotland which has done little to help the competitive swimmers.

However, all is not gloomy. More and more coaches are being employed on a part-time or full-time basis by the swimming clubs. And it is from these clubs, who get little support from the A.S.A.,

David Wilkie, silver medallist in Munich Olympics, gold winner in European championships in Belgrade, is an inspiration to all young British swimmers.

that most of our successful swimmers are emerging. And this is an area of the sport for which the ruling body has created few guidelines.

Thus a situation which has been accepted in America for many years could come about by default in Britain. In the U.S.A. the coach is the most important man or woman in swimming. Next comes the swimmer and supporting the competitive team come the officials. In this way American swimming fame is world-wide. The success spread to diving, water polo, sychronised swimming . . . and ultimately to the encouragement of swimming as a means of saving lives. And surely that is the ambition of the A.S.A.

Now the England swimmers are pleading: 'Let's agree that competitive swimming is the horse that powers the cart . . . even if it is the cart that delivers the goods.'

How sound is the swimmers' argument? Think back to the 1970 Commonwealth Games and the emergence of a young Edinburgh schoolboy as a genuine world-class breast-stroke swimmer and his award of a bronze medal in the 200 metres breast-stroke.

David Wilkie followed this with a silver medal in the 1972 Olympic Games and a world record and gold medal in the first world championships in Belgrade in 1973.

Can anyone doubt that Wilkie's superb achievement of lifting British breast-stroke swimming into world class for the first time in almost fifty years did not influence David Leigh of Sheffield and Paul Naisby of Sunderland, the swimmers who shared with him all the medals in the 100 and 200 metres breast-stroke in the 1974 Commonwealth Games.

There is no doubt in my mind that gold medals, in fact medals of any hue, draw youngsters to swimming. Medals nourish sport.

Critics claim Britain is not capable of producing or attracting coaches of world calibre.

Nonsense. I have only to mention the names of Deryk Snelling and Don Talbot to hear official

A bunch of young swimming belles . . . Joanne Atkinson, Kim Wickham, Penny Beatham and Alyson Jones.

teeth gnashing like a well-worn gearbox.

Deryk was the ultra-successful coach of Southampton who moved to Vancouver. In 1972 he was coach to the Canadian Olympic squad. The following year he was joined by Don Talbot of Australia, an Australian Olympic coach in 1964, 1968 and 1972. Together these vastly experienced and enthusiastic men have created a new feeling and mood in Canada. In the Christchurch Games the Canadians won four of the five team swimming titles and opened the Games by winning all three medals in the women's highboard diving.

So what? Firstly, a more enlightened approach by the Amateur Swimming Association could have kept Snelling in Britain.

Secondly Don Talbot, *en route* to Canada, spoke to swimming officials, coaches, swimmers and writers and said: 'If I receive the right offer I would love to stay in Britain.'

Naturally, the 'right offer' to this successful coach is a question of finance. His offer was dismissed with scant consideration.

When you start watching the swimming events from the 1976 Olympic Games and a new world power is unleashed and the juggernaut that will then be Canadian swimming performing before their own people, think about the two men who could have been wearing British and not Canadian colours.

However with the determination and a new mood unleashed by home country swimmers during the Commonwealth Games, slightly dampened at the European championships, British swimming is slowly improving.

Perhaps our swimmers and especially our coaches have one major failing, due mainly to inexperience and that is a desire to create rather than mould the available material.

I can remember time and again the anger and frustration of Bedford's Brian Brinkley and his coaches Charlie Wilson and Neville Cross. All three were convinced that Brinkley's future lay as a freestyler despite some good butterfly and individual medley swims.

Then dramatically in 1972 Brian furrowed through as a world-class butterfly swimmer. From that moment I was convinced the 200 metres butterfly was Brian's main event. But the Bedford coaching team disagreed. 'Brian,' they claimed, 'was going to be a world freestyle champion – or bust.' He competed in the world championships in 1973 and his best performance . . . fourth place in the 200 metres butterfly.

Then New Zealand and swimming in February, very much outside the British season, Brian was forced to accept his future lay in butterfly.

What changed his mind? Nothing very much, just a gold medal in the 200 metres butterfly. But this is what swimming is all about, gaining experience and accepting that other people might have the right idea about 'your' swimmer.

And will the elders now bow to the wishes of England's young swimmers and coaches?

Not immediately but changes must come. The same group of men have controlled English swimming with little change for almost fifteen years.

Slowly a few are being forced to retire through age. There remains one bulwark which can prevent the real development of competitive swimming in Britain and that is a self-propagating aspect of the A.S.A. Committee. As one long-serving member after another retires a number are being elected life members and allowed a vote at committee meetings.

Until this bulwark is breeched the 'True Blue Amateurism' as envisaged by the current Amateur Swimming Association will always be a hindrance.

This seems a very serious story to tell at Christmas time but if you love sport and swimming the way I do, you'll appreciate the sport is for young people. What is the answer? It is up to the international swimmers of today and yesterday to come into the sport as officials, and not to be frightened to speak their minds.

And lastly, be aware of their own failings and the moment they reach such a barrier just as they reached barriers in their swimming careers then that is the time to bow out gracefully instead of growing old inside what is still one of the world's youngest and most underdeveloped sports.

One thing I can promise and that is world swimming records for years to come. I would also like to be able to promise that British swimmers will figure regularly in the record books! Let's hope the swimmers have their way.

What a trio! David Wilkie (*centre*) wins the gold medal, David Leigh (*left*) takes silver while Paul Naisby lifts the bronze in the Commonwealth Games at Christchurch.

SPORTS QUIZ ANSWERS

Football

1. Manchester City and Wolves.
2. Nothing. He was signed on a free transfer.
3. Blackburn Rovers.
4. England lost 2–0 in Poland and drew 1–1 at Wembley.
5. Three, Spurs, Millwall and Chelsea.
6. Don Gillies.

Table Tennis

1. In London in 1927.
2. Five. The first in 1932.
3. Fred Perry in 1929. Later he became Wimbledon lawn tennis singles champion.
4. Satoh of Japan. He won the title in 1952.
5. Jung Kuo-Tuan – in 1959.
6. In England. The Ping Pong Association.

Cricket

1. Tony Greig.
2. Sixteen.
3. Keith Fletcher.
4. Graham McKenzie.
5. Bev Congdon.
6. Ted Hemsley.

Angling

1. A salmon, sea trout or trout, after hatching from the egg and with a yolk sac suspended from it from which it subsists.
2. An eel, the elver being the baby eel when it comes to British and European shores to enter the rivers.
3. The grayling.
4. The blue, porbeagle and tope.
5. The black bream and the red bream.
6. In sand and sandy mud on the sea-shore, specially on banks near the low water mark.

Golf

1. Johnny Miller.
2. Peter Oosterhuis.
3. Mike Bonallack.
4. Leeds United who play at Wetherby in July for the Don Revie trophy.
5. Jack Nicklaus.
6. The average on a standard size course of 6,500 yards is five miles.

Boxing

1. Joe Frazier and Ken Norton. He beat them both in return fights.
2. Light-middleweight and light-welterweight. Larry Paul and Des Morrison were the first champions of these divisions.
3. Muhammad Ali and Joe Frazier. Bugner lost both fights on points.
4. Ismal Laguna of Puerto Rico in 1970. Roberto Duran (Panama) in 1972.
5. Once. He knocked out Joe Roman in one round.
6. Neville Meade (heavy), Billy Knight (light-heavy) and Pat Cowdell (bantam) for England. David Lamour (fly) for N. Ireland.

Swimming

1. Pat Beavan of Wales who won the 200 metres breaststroke title in a British record time.
2. Cali, Colombia.
3. David Leigh of Sheffield. He won the 100 metres breaststroke with Wilkie second.
4. Shane Gould of Australia.
5. Pat Beavan's husband John, a Welsh baths manager.
6. Yes and No. There will not be another British Commonwealth Games, but there will be a Commonwealth Games. It was agreed during the 1974 Games that the word British be deleted from the title of the Games.